Early Reader's Co~~n~~

The concept of *Intelli*~~gent Vulnerability has been stirring in~~ Chris's heart for many years as he has traveled the path of knowing himself in light of his identity in Christ. Chris shares with us an ancient truth that cannot and should not be ignored. The reality is that there is A Story, and there is also "our story," both of which are inseparable. We must all take the journey into the depths of both stories to experience the truth of what the Gospel reveals about God and what it reveals about us. In doing so we find the ability to live in the trusting innocence our hearts were created for as we no longer need the protective strategies that keep us from fully living into our Kingdom destiny.

Intelligent Vulnerability doesn't just diagnose a problem. It offers a roadmap and guide to help you take this critical journey - with others at your side.

*Bruce A Dodson, Founder
of King and Kingdom Ministries
Licensed Professional Counselor*

This book accurately reflects what it is like being a soul-level friend to the author, Chris Cox. It encapsulates, beautifully, the lessons Chris has taught me over the many years of friendship.

Chris has lived a life that is visually inconsistent with his spirit. I recall sitting in his dorm room in college when a classmate asked him if he wanted to go play basketball with their friends. It is telling that a college-aged boy – who could not participate in simple activities of daily living such as independently bathing, toileting, or walking – was known at such a deep level that he was included in the group activity invitation. His disability was totally forgotten. As Chris describes in his book, his inability to physically participate meant that he worked harder to emotionally be available and carry others' burdens. He taught me how the shell of the physical human does not matter, but instead, if we are lucky, we actually become friends with a person's spirit.

This book teaches us how to form truly soul-level friendships – a skill I have learned personally from the author.

Mary Carole Young Smith, Partner
Munson, Rowlett, Moore, and Boone Law Firm
Special Justice, Arkansas Supreme Court
Trial Attorney, Speaker

In a world where we are bombarded by chaos, insincerity, and too often, misguided teachings that provide little insight towards improving our emotional well-being, *Intelligent Vulnerability: Gate to the Heart* shares insight, perspective, and knowledge that was learned through what I can only call the miraculous journey of life, love, loss, and faith experienced by the author, Mr. Cox. His unique perspective and life are artistically woven with his academia and counseling experience to provide the framework for this challenging and thought-provoking breakdown on how to search within, how to confront insecurity and emotion, and how to safely share yourself with the world around you.

Anthony Sayadian, President
Equity Partners Mortgage

My good friend and brother in Christ has led us all into a solid plan to be whole emotionally, mentally and spiritually. As I read the book, I saw his heart and love for people. He leads us to explore those deeper things that we have spent so many years putting blocks in front of, those things that we have never really been honest about. I will caution you that this is a dangerous read, especially through the questions, because most likely you won't like the answers. I have personally experienced the feeling of the weights being lifted. I know Chris has a passion for Christ and a calling to build up the body. So, if you will let him, he will lead you into more full relationships with people and a more solid relationship with Christ that comes from being complete. Good luck on your journey and God Bless.

Joseph L. Conaway
Ordained bi-vocational minister
Service Advisor, Superior Chevrolet Buick GMC

Chris Cox is one of the most amazing followers of Christ I have ever met in my life or ministry. Living in a world of difficult challenges every moment of his life, Chris faces each test knowing that God is with Him and has called him to this battle for His glory. If you want a real blessing, read this testimony of a man who walks in victory and refuses to be a victim. It will touch the deepest parts of your soul to see his triumphant faith overcoming every fear. To God be the glory....great things He has done through the life of Chris Cox!

Dr. Larry Petton, Senior Pastor
Cross Pointe Community Church
Author

As I read the book, *Intelligent Vulnerability*, I was amazed at the insights the author received while battling both emotional and physical problems as he endeavored to understand the mind of Christ in it all. Refusing to dwell in the depression that engulfs so many others who encounter lesser trials, Chris uses challenges as a means of understanding life, then uses his insights to help others grow in their relationship with Jesus Christ. And with a background in counseling, love for the Lord, and compassion for people, Chris has produced an important resource that should be read by all who battle physical challenges.

S. Eugene Linzey
Author, publisher

I was fortunate to be one of the first readers of this new book written by Chris Cox. Being a family friend and family physician, I witnessed the devastating physical effects of Chris' disability, while also watching the strength and courage he found to persevere. Chris found his faith in God early on and is a powerful witness of God's Grace to people young and old. His faith, education, and life experiences led him to write this book.

Intelligent Vulnerability can be read as a short book to help the reader understand their own vulnerabilities and how to deal with them, or as an in-depth study guide for us individually or for a group study. It includes advice on how to share one's vulnerabilities and how to choose a vulnerability partner This book is based on biblical truths and God's word and the real-life perspective of a powerful man of God living with vulnerabilities in his own life.

Thomas Hollis MD
Fellow American Academy of Family Physicians

Chris Cox is a voice we need in our world today. His words call us to be better and more authentic. His stories are shared as a fellow sojourner in life, but he leads with a teaching heart. Don't miss what's in these pages!

Sarah Harmeyer
Founder, Chief People Gatherer
Neighbor's Table

"If you want to go fast, go alone, if you want to go far, go together." African Proverb

I met Chris Cox soon after his birth, as a patient in my Pediatric Practice. I have been positively impacted by observing this gentle warrior's personal journey of faith. I envision Chris as the iron chosen to become the exquisite, honed, million-layered blade of an ancient Samurai sword. He also quietly yielded himself to destiny. Beautiful comparison? Maybe? Yet, my analogy certainly cannot capture the complexities of Chris's life. Obviously not iron, he's a sentient human, capable of contemplating his own position, pain, progress (gain or loss), and purpose. Chris writes that he first acknowledged that his God uniquely "formed me in my mother's womb to be His servant". He was then forged, not with bellows, furnace, hammer, and anvil, but in God's providential will, by individuals, relationships, and his insights, perfected and then practiced. Chris writes, first using familiar terms, concepts from his profession.

He exquisitely interweaves Biblical truths with them, and suddenly we discover something unique. He is guiding us toward understanding a more nearly perfect therapeutic modality, new, but essential in our quest for wholeness. He's willing to use it upon himself, where he discovers, refines, and applies this new modality to his own journey. In doing so, the "iron" works with the "blacksmith", and Chris, in God's providence, His Word, and by intelligently making himself vulnerable. Intelligent Vulnerability uniquely moves us toward wholeness. I'll read it and again!

Jon M. Robert, MD

In this intimate and insightful personal account Chris reminds us that we are uniquely created by God for relationships. He lays a Scriptural foundation for discovering and choosing vulnerability as God's path to a fulfilling life. If you desire to know peace and joy in all circumstances then prepare to be challenged and inspired.

Manley Beasley Jr., Senior Pastor,
Hot Springs Baptist Church

In Intelligent Vulnerability: Gate to the Heart, Chris Cox shares insight from his own personal life experiences to inspire, encourage, and challenge readers to find a deeper understanding of themselves and their relationships. Having been fraternity brothers and living across the hall from Chris in college, this book provides great insight into what I already knew to be a courageous and inspiring life. The perspective that Chris shares based upon the truth of the Gospel has application for all.

Matthew J. Shepherd, Speaker of the House
Arkansas House of Representatives

Intelligent Vulnerability:

Gate to the Heart

Intelligent Vulnerability:

Gate to the Heart

Chris Cox

P & L Publishing
& Literary Services

Intelligent Vulnerability: Gate to the Heart
Copyright © 2023 Chris Cox
Cover Design by Rendi Threadgill
Published in the United States of America.

All rights reserved. No portion of this book may be reproduced, stored in a retrieval system, or transmitted in any form or by any means – electronic, mechanical, photocopy, recording, or any other – except for brief quotations in critical reviews or articles without the prior permission of the author.

Scriptures taken from the Holy Bible, New International Version®, NIV®. Copyright © 1973, 1978, 1984, 2011 by Biblica, Inc.™ Used by permission of Zondervan.

ISBN: 9798871047286

Dedication

To my dad:

You left this earth far too early. However, you left an imprint on my heart that will last forever. I will always be grateful that you encouraged me to never let an obstacle stand in the way of reaching my hopes and dreams. Until we meet again in Heaven.

To my mom:

I thrived and soared because of your unconditional love, support, and prayers every day of my life. I love you both more than words can express.

Contents

Dedication xi
Preface xv
Section 1 The Foundation for Intelligent Vulnerability 1
1 My Diagnosis, Transparency, and Vulnerability 3
2 Created for Intimate Relationships 15
3 Spin, Walls, and Desire for Connection 31
4 Motives for Emotional Vulnerability 39
Section 2 The Process of Intelligent Vulnerability 53
5 Recognizing Our Vulnerabilities 55
6 Which Road Do I Take? 69
7 Confronting Our Vulnerabilities 85
8 Are You Ready? Three Big Questions 97
9 How Do You Know Who to Trust? 113
Section 3 Tips, Purposes, and Proofs IV Works 127
10 Some Important Tips 129
11 Freedom, Oneness, and Faith 141
12 The Rest of My Story 157
Acknowledgements 173

Preface

I suffer from early-onset Facioscapulohumeral Muscular Dystrophy and rely on a power wheelchair for mobility. As a total care patient in the medical field, I require assistance with basic tasks like dressing, toileting, bathing, and feeding. Despite my condition, my life is fulfilling and rich.

After completing my undergraduate studies in Christian Counseling and Psychology at Ouachita Baptist University, I pursued a master's degree in Christian Counseling at Denver Seminary. Following my graduation, I returned to Hot Springs, Arkansas, where I became a Licensed Associate Counselor and later a Licensed Professional Counselor. I spent five years working in private practice before transitioning to Community Counseling Services, where I worked for seven years as a group therapist in their day treatment program for the chronically mentally ill. Due to health issues, I eventually decided to retire from my profession.

I've been happily married to my lovely wife, Lisa, for 16 years. Together, we have two wonderful children named Caitlan and Ayden. We live a fulfilling life that revolves around our church, spending time with loved ones, and watching our favorite shows.

As you can see, I am living a blessed life despite my disability, however, I spent the first 22 years of my life in denial, pretending that my disability didn't matter. I used my faith in God to hide from the real emotions that surrounded my disability. This book focuses on the next 3 years of my life where God challenged me to quit hiding and confront my deepest emotions concerning this vulnerability.

As I reflect on a significant period in my life, I have come to realize that the knowledge and skills I gained may be useful to others. By combining my background in counseling with my passion for the Bible, I have developed a concept that I call Intelligent Vulnerability. It was not a realization that I reached on my own, as I have discussed my thoughts with many individuals over the years. However, I must give special recognition to Jimmie Reed, who first helped me to articulate my ideas and put them down in writing 15 years ago. I am grateful for the time and effort he invested in me, which served as the foundation for my book.

As you read further, I hope to inspire, encourage, and challenge you. I will share my personal journey of confronting my deepest emotions related to my disability, which illustrates the Intelligent Vulnerability process outlined in this book. Through this process, I discovered how to heal, gain freedom, and build more intimate relationships. While there are no guarantees in life, I am confident that you too can safely confront your own emotions. It may not be easy and will take time, but if you follow the process, you can also experience healing, freedom, and deeper connections. Now, let's begin!

Section 1

The Foundation for Intelligent Vulnerability

1
My Diagnosis, Transparency, and Vulnerability

May 20, 1977, was no ordinary day in the Cox family. Around midmorning, a beautiful baby boy was born to Randy and Brenda Cox. I was their first child, and they were proud parents. I began walking at eight months and was an early developer in many ways. My parents have often said that I loved playing ball ever since I was old enough to hold or throw one. A little over two years later, my brother, Robbie, was born. We both loved playing ball together. My parents felt blessed to have two healthy boys, and life was good.

That all began changing when I was about four years old and ran up to my mom and said, "Mommy, mommy, will you hold my lips so I can blow up the balloons like the other kids?" This was one of the small things that my parents began noticing was not normal for my age. I was unable to close my eyelids tightly or smile big.

The doctors initially thought that I may have had a virus in utero that caused nerve damage to my face, but as things got worse over the next couple of years, my parents decided to have the doctors look more closely. After a muscle biopsy, doctors came to a more daunting diagnosis, Facioscapulohumeral Muscular Dystrophy. I was only six years old, and the doctors told my parents there was no treatment and no cure. We were told to go home and live life the best we could.

My parents were shocked. Now, everything was changing, and they had no idea what this new diagnosis would mean for us. My dad would later tell me that he was devastated and went into denial for the next two years. However, there had been a poem on the wall in the hospital that stuck with both mom and dad. It was "Footprints in the Sand" by Mary Stevenson. The one that talks about God carrying us through the most difficult times in life.

This new diagnosis brought my parents to their knees in prayer and brought a deeper conviction that they needed the Lord as their refuge. They knew that they needed to find their strength in God and trust that He was going to carry them in those times when life became too difficult. They have told me since, that it was years before they truly surrendered me into the Lord's hands. This surrender often takes time and requires us to deepen our walk with the Lord and mature in our faith and trust.

My parents believed that despite my diagnosis, I was a normal boy and chose to treat me as such. They were determined not to do anything for me that I was able to do for myself. My parents had no idea to what extent I would be affected by this muscular dystrophy, but they knew that for me to be successful I would have to learn determination and perseverance. They knew I would not learn these qualities if they pampered me. My parents taught me to look at obstacles and see them as challenges to overcome, and I am grateful for the wisdom they used in raising me.

I continued living my life the only way I knew how. I was a natural athlete; that's what people told me. In kindergarten, I was the runner who came from behind to help win a 4x40 relay for my class. I was always the quarterback at recess because I could throw the touchdown pass.

By the fifth grade, I had a foot brace on my right leg and could only run about half as fast as the other kids, but I still pitched and played second base for my pony league team. I remember my dad telling me, "You may not be the hardest thrower, but all you do is throw strikes!" On the other hand, there was a time or two that I would hit the ball to the fence and get thrown out at first base. None of that mattered because I loved playing the game and being out there with my friends.

This was the last year I was able to play organized sports because we chose to have surgery on my right Achilles tendon. After I got the cast off from the surgery, my calf muscle had seriously diminished, and I was no longer able to run anymore. I remember being disappointed that I had to stop playing baseball. I never fully recovered from that surgery. I seemingly took these major letdowns in stride and never made a big deal out of them, but I became an expert at using my faith in God to hide from the real emotions that surrounded my disability. You will hear stories in future chapters about me finally confronting them and finding healing in my early 20s.

You will also see how I learned to be vulnerable to selected people, in a safe way, and how those relationships played the primary role in me finding healing to some of my deepest vulnerabilities. I have termed this method Intelligent Vulnerability.

Transparency vs. Vulnerability

I have purposely chosen to begin by sharing some of my stories with you partly because my story is woven throughout the chapters to help illustrate how Intelligent Vulnerability brought healing to some of my deepest vulnerabilities. But I also chose stories that I can share with anyone because they show transparency, not vulnerability.

So, what do you think of when you hear the words transparency and vulnerability? What do you think the difference is between these two words?

Transparency and vulnerability are two key words that we will follow throughout the remainder of this book. It is vital that we understand them and differentiate between them, because many times in our culture people use these two concepts interchangeably, by mistake. For the purpose of this book, we will distinguish between emotional transparency and emotional vulnerability.

Let's first look at the word *transparent*. Merriam-Webster defines transparent as "easily detected or seen through." Another definition is "free from deceit." For our purposes, emotional transparency could simply be defined as *sharing an aspect of ourselves, with minimal risk, because there is no invitation for another person to come inside our emotional wall*. We let others see the obvious, but we don't invite them behind our wall. Have you ever opened the door of your home, just a little, to see who is there? Normally, unless we know the person, we keep the conversation at the door.

Everything I have shared with you up to this point would come under this definition of emotional transparency. I have shared with you an overview of the first part of my life, but I have yet to show you some of the inner workings of my heart. It has been safe and surface-level for the most part. I have maintained complete control of what I have been sharing. You know a little bit more about me, yet you still don't know me.

Now let's look at the word *vulnerable*. Merriam-Webster defines vulnerable as "capable of being physically or emotionally wounded." Another definition is "open to attack or damage."

Emotional vulnerability is *sharing a more sensitive aspect of ourselves that involves an element of significant risk because we have invited someone to come inside—behind our wall to see us as we really are*. We not only let them peek in through our door, but we invite them in to know more.

Throughout the remainder of this book, I will invite you to come inside behind the wall, and I will share with you one of my greatest vulnerabilities in which I found healing. I will share stories that were extremely sensitive and required great risk at the time. You will find out in the pages of this book that while I have grown tremendously over my life, I am by no means a finished product. As new stages of my life unfold, there are new aspects concerning my vulnerabilities that I must continually bring before the Lord and those I trust the most.

So, what about you? Are you willing to share yourself with those around you? Do you know how? Can you do it safely? Intelligently? You may be thinking that you can handle being transparent, but you're not so sure about this "vulnerability stuff." It is my belief that we all have a desire to be known and to know, but it's scary and risky.

We might be thinking, "If you really knew some of the thoughts that run through my mind or some of the issues I struggle with, you would surely leave and not want to be around me again."

Let me ask, how many people know details about your life? Now, how many people know intimate details of your heart? This is the difference between transparency and vulnerability.

I would venture to guess that very few of us have the courage to let those around us truly know us. In fact, along with the reality that we are scared to share deeply, many of us don't truly know ourselves. We need to learn what it means to truly come to know ourselves and be known by those closest to us. We will uncover this mystery by learning how to be appropriately and Intelligently Vulnerable.

We can't be an open book to everyone all the time; we must protect ourselves. This is where the intelligent part comes in.

As children, most of us had desires, hopes, and dreams for the future. Some of us dreamed of being Superman, Spiderman, Wonder Woman, or some other superhero. Others of us dreamed of being a sports star, movie star, or somebody famous. Maybe you hoped for that fairytale marriage, with perfect kids, and an easy life. Or hoped that you would grow up to change the world. But somewhere along the way, we became disillusioned. We grew up and reality set in. We realized that life isn't easy or fair. While there are many amazing and wonderful parts to life, there is also pain, sickness, disease, and heartbreak. People let us down. We find that money can't buy happiness. We see that our perfect spouse isn't quite so perfect, and neither are we. Some people deal with health issues, cancer, addiction, assault, disability, mental illness, or a plethora of other situations. We realized that life hurts sometimes, often too deeply for words when things don't turn out the way we hoped, dreamed, or expected.

So, what do we do? We usually look to ourselves to find a way to cope with it. We choose to lower our expectations, to lessen the blow of being disappointed. We build walls to protect ourselves from the world around us. In doing so, we settle for much less than what God intended for us. We now look for other means to meet our need to feel connected to those around us.

In our culture, it is normal to enjoy reading a good book or watching a good movie. What is it that you enjoy about this the most? The plot? The romance? The action? The fantasy? What kind of emotions do you feel? Love? Excitement? Inspiration? Compassion? Anger? Suspense? Sadness? Fear?

Now let's go even deeper and much more personal. Do you connect with your spouse or your loved ones the way you connect with those characters in that book or on that movie screen? Books and movies are written to make you feel emotions and connect with the characters. Most of us don't have as much trouble opening ourselves up to deep emotions when they don't directly affect us. There is very little risk involved because those characters on that screen or in that book don't have the ability to interact with us. They can't hurt us, laugh at us, or disappoint us. So, it doesn't really require us to be vulnerable. It's a very safe, risk-free way for us to allow ourselves to feel at a deep level. We call this entertainment, and it has a purpose to serve. But it should never replace real-life connection and intimacy. This is a cheap imitation of the kind of intimate relationships that God intends for us.

What does this intimate relationship look like, this relationship where I am truly known and I truly know, this kind of relationship that God intends for us and how can we get it? Well, as in any good book, I can't give you all my secrets in the first chapter. But I will tell you that the key is Intelligent Vulnerability.

Closing Thought

I want to lay down a challenge for you. We are always changing, but few of us are always growing. Not one of us stays exactly how we are right now. Sadly, the only change we see in some people is that they are becoming more and more entrenched in their own stubborn mindsets. These are often the same people who say "This is just who I am, I can't help it. You deal with it. You change." On the other hand, some people are willing to confront their shortcomings or insecurities and grow towards becoming a better person.

This book is not just intended to help you learn how Intelligent Vulnerability can help you build the kind of deeply intimate relationships that you were created for. The purpose begins at a far more basic place. It begins with each of us being willing to look at ourselves in a more honest way in which we respond by making a concerted effort to grow towards becoming a better person. Which person will you choose to be? Your choice will directly affect how much value this book will have in your life.

If you are ready to know and be known by those closest to you, if you are ready to find healing for your vulnerabilities, if you are ready to start seeing yourself as God sees you, then the rest of this book may be for you. One of the best ways that I have discovered to find these answers is through the exercise of what I call Intelligent Vulnerability–two small words, one huge implication.

Key Concepts

Emotional transparency - sharing an aspect of ourselves with minimal risk because there is no invitation for another person to come inside our emotional wall.

Emotional vulnerability - sharing a more sensitive aspect of ourselves that involves an element of significant risk because we have invited someone to come inside—behind our wall to see us as we really are.

We can't be an open book to everyone because not everyone is safe. We must protect ourselves.

Discussion points (Group)

Can you explain the difference between transparency and vulnerability?

How many people are you emotionally transparent with?

How many people are you emotionally vulnerable with?

Is there a difference in the quality of the relationships between the two?

Is some level of emotional vulnerability necessary for life?

Do you need to learn how to be safer when sharing these deeper emotions?

Do you desire to be more deeply connected to those closest to you?

Are you willing to share yourself with those around you?

Getting personal (Just for you)

Do you know yourself, your inner emotions?

What are some of your hopes and dreams?

Have you lowered your expectations to lessen the blow of being disappointed?

Who and what has disappointed you?
Are you willing to grow and change?
Do you desire to be a better version of yourself?
If so, are you willing to put in the work required?
Are you ready to know and be known by those closest to you?

2
Created for Intimate Relationships

We talked about hopes, desires, and dreams of our childhood, but then we became disillusioned. We talked about how reality set in, and the world is often a harsh and unfair place to live. We found out that it hurt, sometimes badly, when things didn't turn out the way we thought they would. So, what do we do? We lower our expectations to lessen the blow of disappointment. And in doing, so we settle for much less than what God intended for us in the beginning.

God intended for us to develop relationships

What exactly is it that God intended?

Let us look together at Genesis 1:26-31 and find out what God's Word tells us.

Gen 1:26 "Then God said, "Let us make mankind in our image, in our likeness, so that they may rule over the fish in the sea and the birds in the sky, over the livestock and all the wild animals, and over all the creatures that move along the ground." 27 So God created mankind in his own image, in the image of God he created them; male and female he created them. 28 God blessed them and said to them, "Be fruitful and increase in number; fill the earth and subdue it. Rule over the fish in the sea and the birds in the sky and over every living creature that moves on the ground." 29 Then God said, "I give you every seed-bearing plant on the face of the whole earth and every tree that has fruit with seed in it. They will be yours for food. 30 And to all the beasts of the earth and all the birds in the sky and all the creatures that move along the ground—everything that has the breath of life in it—I give every green plant for food." And it was so. 31 God saw all that he had made, and it was very good. And there was evening, and there was morning—the sixth day."

God created man in his likeness and gave them a special place over all creation. We read in verse 28 that God blessed them and told them to have children and enjoy all that the world has to offer. Wow! What an amazing plan that was, and what an incredible God we serve, to desire such things for us. As we read on, we see that everything He created was very good.

Can you imagine what life must have been like? I sit and think about how many beautiful landscapes, sunsets, and sunrises we get to experience in our fallen world and wonder how much more glorious God's creation was in the beginning. Adam lived in a world in which there was no sin, sickness, or disease. There was no pain, no heartache, and no death. He would walk and talk with God and was in total communion with Him. The Lord had placed within Adam a desire for an intimate connection with his maker.

Something is still missing

Isn't it interesting that even though Adam had all these things, still something was missing? So, what was missing?

Let's look at Genesis 2:18-25.

Gen 2:18 "The Lord God said, "It is not good for the man to be alone. I will make a helper suitable for him." 19 Now the Lord God had formed out of the ground all the wild animals and all the birds in the sky. He brought them to the man to see what he would name them; and whatever the man called each living creature, that was its name. 20 So the man gave names to all the livestock, the birds in the sky and all the wild animals. But for Adam[f] no suitable helper was found.

21 So the Lord God caused the man to fall into a deep sleep; and while he was sleeping, he took one of the man's ribs[g] and then closed up the place with flesh. 22 Then the Lord God made a woman from the rib[h] he had taken out of the man, and he brought her to the man. 23 The man said, "This is now bone of my bones and flesh of my flesh; she shall be called 'woman,' for she was taken out of man." 24 That is why a man leaves his father and mother and is united to his wife, and they become one flesh. 25 Adam and his wife were both naked, and they felt no shame."

We see here that Adam was missing Eve as a helpmate. Adam must have been excited when he awoke to find a woman by his side. God had created in Adam a desire to be intimately connected with another human being. From the very beginning, we were created to intimately know both God and one another. This need for intimate relationships has been placed in us by God Almighty himself. True intimacy is indeed a gift from God.

What characteristics do you think this kind of relationship would have?
- trust
- acceptance
- love
- communication

If God created us with this need to be intimately connected to one another, then why do we live in a world that is often isolated and lonely with many superficial and unfulfilling relationships?

What happened

Let's look back to Genesis 3:1-13 to find our answer.

Gen 3:1 "Now the serpent was more crafty than any of the wild animals the Lord God had made. He said to the woman, "Did God really say, 'You must not eat from any tree in the garden'?" 2 The woman said to the serpent, "We may eat fruit from the trees in the garden, 3 but God did say, 'You must not eat fruit from the tree that is in the middle of the garden, and you must not touch it, or you will die.'" 4 "You will not certainly die," the serpent said to the woman. 5 "For God knows that when you eat from it your eyes will be opened, and you will be like God, knowing good and evil." 6 When the woman saw that the fruit of the tree was good for food and pleasing to the eye, and also desirable for gaining wisdom, she took some and ate it. She also gave some to her husband, who was with her, and he ate it. 7 Then the eyes of both of them were opened, and they realized they were naked; so, they sewed fig leaves together and made coverings for themselves. 8 Then the man and his wife heard the sound of the Lord God as he was walking in the garden in the cool of the day, and they hid from the Lord God among the trees of the garden. 9 But the Lord God called to the man, "Where are you?" 10 He answered, "I heard you in the garden, and I was afraid because I was naked; so, I hid." 11 And he said, "Who told you that you were naked? Have you eaten from the tree that I commanded you not to eat from?" 12 The man said, "The woman you put here with me—she gave me some fruit from the tree, and I ate it." 13 Then the Lord God said to the woman, "What is this you have done?" The woman said, "The serpent deceived me, and I ate."

Adam and Eve were tempted by the devil and chose to disobey God. This choice brought sin into the world, and amid the sin, something very precious was lost...Trust. Adam and Eve no longer trusted God to do what was best for them. They liked what Satan offered and made the choice to ignore God's command and follow Satan. This ended up with trust being broken between Adam and Eve, with him blaming her and her blaming the serpent. So, trust was lost, and we gained a few new things Adam and Eve had never experienced before, such as shame, fear, and blame. There would now be a huge chasm in our ability to be intimately connected with God and with one another. That intimacy we once shared naturally, now requires great work.

God created Adam and had an intimate relationship with him. He allowed Adam to live for a time without Eve so that he would feel and realize his need for her. And then Adam got to experience the difference of living life with an intimate mate. God put Adam and Eve in a perfect world with great responsibilities, and life was good.

But then came Satan, the true enemy of every person's soul, to tempt Adam and Eve to choose to follow him over God. We know what happened. They followed Satan. The choice that they made changed their entire world. They went from intimacy with God and each other, in innocence and purity, where there were no vulnerabilities, but just love and trust, to being plunged into a dark and confusing world with shame, fear, blame, and death. They were now naked, ashamed, guilty, blaming, and vulnerable, trusting nobody. God stopped the daily walks and talks in the garden. They had to pack up and move out of the perfect garden and go figure it out on their own.

As Adam and Eve ate the forbidden fruit, everything changed, including the way we view ourselves. For the first time, we became self-reflective and could evaluate and make judgments about ourselves and others. It was here that we became aware of our inadequacies, flaws, and differences. We were no longer clothed in God's glory but rather decided we must try to clothe ourselves. At this moment, the spin-self was born.

The spin-self is a term I came up with. It is a mechanism that many of us use that continually manages our self-image by "spinning" information because we chose to disobey God and now look to ourselves for protection instead of Him. Since we are no longer protected by God, we choose to look out for ourselves because we certainly can't trust others to. Self-protection is one of the primary roles our spin-self takes over. It tells us nobody else will protect us, so we had better figure out how to do it. We no longer trust that God knows what's best for us, so we have come up with our own solution. Even after we've been reconciled back to God through Christ, we still struggle with this. Every time we sin, we are making a choice that our way is better than God's way. The spin-self uses anything it can, especially deception, to protect us from being exposed or to help us avoid taking responsibility for our actions.

We see right here in this passage exactly how the spin-self works. Adam and Eve knew they had disobeyed God, so what did they do? We read in Genesis 3:7-8 that they preceded to cover themselves in fig leaves and then tried to hide from the Lord. Hiding from God, who knows everything!

Let's look at verse 10 to see what it says. It tells us that Adam was afraid because he was naked, so he hid. Then in verse, 11 God asks, *"Who told you that you were naked?"* God knew what had transpired, and he knew the consequences they would face. Adam immediately responded with something that we know all too well.

He blamed Eve and Eve in turn blamed the devil. Do you see how the spin-self works? It will use any tool at its disposal to spin information for our protection. As we'll see in the coming chapters, sometimes the spinning is directed outwardly to protect us from others, but there are times when it's directed inwardly to hide our vulnerabilities from ourselves.

Mankind's default position is now for us to see ourselves as the ones responsible for our protection and our lives. Like Adam and Eve, we assume the responsibility for ourselves—knowing good and evil. The weight of the decision-making has become our own. Apart from God, our care has become our own. In a world of similarly flawed people, we find we must protect ourselves from others like us. We hide, we are ashamed, we fear, and we blame. So, our spin-self gets to work and begins building a wall around our hearts to control information about us and to keep people out.

This is our way of protecting ourselves from being vulnerable and facing our faults and the truth. You can see it so clearly in this text. Adam, when questioned by God, blames Eve, and Eve in turn blames the serpent. Oh, how familiar we are with this age-old excuse, "It's not my fault, it's theirs." We began using it as a small child and are still prone to use it all our lives.

You see, before sin entered and trust was broken, we had no need to protect ourselves. There was no danger of being hurt. We didn't even have the ability to make a judgment or evaluate ourselves, because our complete identity was in God. We maintained an intimate and unique relationship with God. We can see from Genesis 3 that Adam and Eve would walk and talk with the Lord in the cool of the day. I can hardly imagine what a beautiful experience that must have been.

Adam and Eve had never given any thought to being transparent or vulnerable. They had no reason to hide anything because sin had not yet come into the world. They were naked and unashamed. Think about it, to be completely accepted just as you are! When we read this text, we usually think about their physical nakedness, but even more profound is that they were also emotionally and spiritually naked, yet unashamed. They had nothing to hide.

But, in one moment, they made a choice to disobey God, and in doing so, they changed the way we would see ourselves and interact with one another. We lost our innocence and would pay a huge price for this choice. The implications of the choice reach far beyond the scope of this book, but we will briefly look at the relational consequences we now face.

The biggest and most profound loss was that the Lord withdrew from us, and we could no longer relate directly to him. (Of course, God had a plan to send Jesus to rescue us from Satan's power over us one day in the future.) We were created for intimacy with God, but our sin separates us from him. Adam and Eve had to work through marital problems for the first time. The blame game took a toll on their trust in each other, you can be sure! Trust between people would continue to be broken and must be earned back over time through shared experiences. We work to build trust by creating multiple positive interactions, experiences, and time spent, while limiting the negative ones. This is the only way to rebuild the bridge of trust, which is necessary to allow us to become intimate once again.

But praise God that we don't have to work our way back to Him. In fact, there is no way to earn back God's trust or His love through our works. Isaiah 64:6 says, *"All of us have become like one who is unclean, and all our righteous acts are like filthy rags."* We are only reconciled to God through the atoning sacrifice of Jesus Christ on the Cross of Calvary.

Romans 10:9 tells us *"If you declare with your mouth, "Jesus is Lord," and believe in your heart that God raised him from the dead, you will be saved."* This, and only this, restores our ability to be intimate with the Lord again.

We were also created as social beings with a need for intimacy with others. Yet, we find that since trust was broken and sin entered, along with shame, fear, and blame, we must protect ourselves from other people too—sometimes even from those whom we love. This means relational intimacy now requires significant risk. In fact, it would, no doubt, be naive and maybe even destructive to trust just anyone with your deepest emotions: those sometimes-unbearable fears and insecurities, those precious hopes and dreams. The spin-self tries its best to keep people from getting too close so that we don't get hurt. But, as we will see, this also means that few people get the opportunity to truly know us.

Managing threats to our hearts

By the time we reach young adulthood, our spin-self has learned to manage quite well. The spin is continually adjusted as the threats change. In doing so, our spin-self keeps us self-centered.

So, what is the answer? What do people do? We usually turn to our own salvation.

We make excuses for ourselves. We say things such as, "If only I were taller, skinnier, or better looking, then life would be so much better" or, "If I only had more money, a better job, or more respect, life would be so much easier" or, "If I could only have more time, energy, or sleep, then life might be more bearable." Excuses do nothing but keep us from the opportunity to embrace and live our lives to the fullest.

We try to "fit in." We see this quite distinctly in teenagers who absolutely must wear the "cool" clothing, or can't live without that latest gadget, along with the age-old quote, "But everyone else is doing it." And it's not just teenagers who have this tendency. As adults, we may realize that just because everyone else is doing it doesn't make it right, but we come up with more sophisticated ways to play the same old games. Maybe this sounds familiar: I need a bigger house or a nicer car so my peers will think I'm successful. I can't save or give a dime to charity because I'm up to my ears in debt.

Sometimes we withdraw and avoid people or situations. We decide that it is too difficult to let people inside. We have the mindset that they are just going to let us down or disappoint us anyway, so why even take the chance? It's easier to keep to ourselves and not risk being hurt yet again. This often leads to our next solution.

We try to "do" or "be." We may throw ourselves into our job to the point where it begins to define us, to where being successful preoccupies our thoughts and it becomes what we live for. All our time, energy, and effort go into work while our relationships, marriages, and kids sit suffering by the wayside. We may even embrace a cause or ideology with which we can identify. This may be a little nobler, but it is no less devastating if we allow it to define who we are.

We know that these things are not unhealthy activities. It is good to desire to improve ourselves; our job helps provide for our families, we all need some time to ourselves, and many causes bring about positive change in the world we live in. The problem is that our spin-self tells us that the world thinks we are not enough without these things. It tells us that the more successful we are, the more people will admire and respect us. It tells us that if we can surround ourselves with the appearance of success, we can hide our brokenness and loneliness from the world around us. The problem is we quickly learn that the only way to make this work is to continue accumulating more and more and doing more and more. And the more we accumulate, the more we need.

If we are wise, then we will learn from the life of Solomon who had more wealth than you could imagine. Listen to his words at the end of his life when he stated in Ecclesiastes 12:8,13-14:

8 "Meaningless! Meaningless!" says the Teacher. "Everything is meaningless!"

13 "Now all has been heard; here is the conclusion of the matter: Fear God and keep his commandments, for this is the duty of all mankind. 14 For God will bring every deed into judgment, including every hidden thing whether it is good or evil."

Maybe you, like Solomon, have come to the point in your life where you realize that striving for material possessions is meaningless. You are tired of listening to the lies of the spin-self and hiding from those you love the most. You desire to live a life that is full of meaning. If this is you, then you may fit into this next solution.

At some point, we realized that what we were doing wasn't working. It's here that we often begin looking for answers outside of ourselves. We begin seeking direction or advice from friends, family, societal icons, or self-help books. Perhaps, we realize we have the need and the courage to reach out for help in the way of professional counseling. These solutions are much better than the ones previously mentioned, but they too are not the end-all-be-all. Because wouldn't you know it, about the time we think we've got it all worked out—we face new or unexpected circumstances forcing us to work it out again.

The reality is that over our lifetime we slowly construct and reconstruct the walls around our hearts, sometimes shutting out family, friends, and even God. Over our lifetime, these walls will take many forms and make many adjustments as we search for some kind of equilibrium between who we are, who we think we are, and who we pretend to be. One thing we come to realize is that we are anything but free. The voice of the spin-self never lets us rest from its accusatory rhetoric.

But all is not lost! This book is not the answer, but I pray that it will lead you to the only answer—Jesus Christ. He has made a way to restore our fellowship with him on the Cross of Calvary. Upon his death, the veil in the temple was torn from top to bottom symbolizing that we would no longer need a mediator between us and God. We can now come before him because Jesus paid the price for our sins. All you have to do is accept his sacrifice on the cross and commit your life to Him. You can once again experience that intimate relationship with our Lord. If we look to him, he will also show us how we can develop intimate relationships with one another.

So let me ask you a question. What would your life be like if you were surrounded by intimate relationships that encouraged your strengths and gently challenged you to grow in those areas of weakness? These are the kinds of relationships that God intends for us.

What kind of relationships can we expect? Do you believe we can still have truly intimate, meaningful, and fulfilling relationships? My answer is an adamant yes! I believe the key to finding these relationships starts with Christ but continues in the process of something I call Intelligent Vulnerability. You don't have to know the Lord to benefit from this book, but it sure helps. We will learn together how appropriate; Intelligent Vulnerability leads to healing, and builds over time, the deeper and more intimate relationships we are created for.

I hope you will come along with me on this amazing and challenging journey as we seek to discover the process of Intelligent Vulnerability.

Key Concepts

We were created for intimate relationships both with God and with one another. But when they chose to disobey God, sin entered the world, and trust was broken. This altered our relationship with God and greatly damaged our relationships with one another.

The spin-self is a mechanism that many of us use that continually manages our self-image by "spinning" information because we chose to disobey God and now look to ourselves for protection instead of Him.

Our spin-self works to build a wall around our hearts to control information about us and to keep people out.

We work to build trust by creating multiple positive interactions, experiences, and time spent, while limiting the negative ones.

Discussion points (Group)

Why do we struggle to have intimate relationships?

Do you believe most relationships today are mainly superficial? Why or why not?

What does it mean to settle for relationships that are less than what God intended for you?

How do we typically protect ourselves from others?

What kind of relationships can we expect now?

Do most people believe we can still have truly intimate, meaningful, and fulfilling relationships?

Getting personal (Just for you)

Can you identify any areas in your life where you "spin" information to protect yourself?

What do you try to hide from God?

Do you tend to blame others when things don't go according to plan?

What excuses do you make for your shortcomings?

Do you trust others easily? If not, who or what has caused you to struggle to trust?

3
Spin, Walls, and Desire for Connection

We have seen in Scripture that God created us with a need for intimate relationships where we are loved and accepted both with Himself and one another. I will venture to say that even though we all search for this, very few of us find it. The reason is that many of us don't know how to build these kinds of relationships. Notice I used the word build. These kinds of relationships take a tremendous amount of time and effort to develop. Most of us pursue relationships in the way that society has taught us or in the way that we say comes "naturally." The problem is that we live in a fallen world, and we are a fallen people with a sinful nature; therefore, although our desires may be legitimate, our ways of finding and maintaining these relationships are incomplete and inaccurate at best. We don't "naturally" know how to build relationships in which we are completely loved and accepted. What comes "naturally" is the old, ugly spin-self that hates the idea of vulnerability.

I think it's fair to say that each one of us has a desire, despite the risk, to have intimate relationships where we know and are known. We also understand that this requires vulnerability.

Emotional Vulnerability. We've defined it, we've talked about it, but do we understand it? Where is it that our vulnerabilities, those deepest emotions, reside? This might be the easiest question I ask in the entire book, and of course, you answered, "our hearts."

Our heart is where our humanity resides—our hopes and dreams, our desire to love and be loved, our desire to know and be known. It's also where our emotional baggage is stashed. That place of our disappointments, put-downs, broken relationships, abuse, broken promises, unforgiveness, anger, fears, inadequacies, unfulfilled dreams, guilt, shame, embarrassment, weaknesses, and failures reside. The list can go on and on. These are rooted in the depths of who we are—where the stakes are the highest and the potential for pain is the greatest.

All our vulnerabilities have tremendous value because they are a part of us. Every person is inherently valuable. And because we are so valuable, this area where our deepest emotions reside must be protected.

So how do we try to protect ourselves? Well, our spin-self builds a wall, a barrier, to try to keep us safe. It's the same concept cities used to use to protect the town from being easily attacked.

Building walls

It is important that we discuss, in a little more detail, the wall that the spin-self builds. God didn't create us with the need for walls. Remember, before the fall we were naked and unashamed, but now as fallen persons, we have no idea how to live without them. We need our walls like we need oxygen. The spin-self tells us we can't survive without our walls, that we will be devoured, and thrown to the wolves without them. There is truth in that statement. Sometimes Christians get this idea that when we come to Jesus, we are supposed to drop all our defenses and become an open book for all to see. It's often camouflaged with ideas of being "genuine" or "building true community." Now don't get me wrong, both words are important to the Christian faith, but they need to be used in the proper context. Nowhere in the Bible does it say we must open our deep, innermost thoughts and experiences for all to see. In fact, Proverbs 4:23 says *"Above all else, guard your heart, for everything you do flows from it."*

The Bible recognizes that our heart is very important and valuable enough, that it's worth guarding. We often use this analogy of our heart to help us explain many of the emotions we feel inside.

The spin-self tells us we better build these walls big and strong. We need to protect ourselves from allowing others to see us, or we will surely be found out. It tells us nobody will like us or accept us if they can see who we really are. So, we listen and build walls as a way of guarding our hearts. The walls give us a sense of protection and peace of mind. They make us feel safe but often keep us from the more intimate relationships we desire.

We continue to add blocks to our wall every time we experience disappointments, put-downs, let-downs, abuse, broken relationships, people taking advantage of us, shattered trust, and many other negative events. The more times we are hurt or taken advantage of, the more blocks we add to our walls and the more valuable they seem to us. So, we build our walls even taller and thicker.

Take some time now and take a personal inventory. What has influenced you to place more blocks on your wall? If you had the courage to write these down, then keep this list in a safe place.

We all desire connection with others

Many of us have wounds and scars because we have opened our hearts and let people behind our walls. This often occurs when we share with the wrong people, or we do it with improper motives. Herein lies the problem with emotional vulnerability, with sharing the depths of our hearts.

When it is done inappropriately and unintelligently, we are left trying to pick up the pieces. Sometimes we decide the pain is just too great to risk letting someone into our hearts again. So, we build these walls to protect ourselves from being hurt again, and we find ourselves in a relatively safe, yet extremely lonely and isolated place.

The desire for connection plus Emotional Vulnerability, when handled inappropriately, often leads to pain which causes us to add blocks to our walls. This results in a tendency to keep relationships safe and shallow.

I am convinced that despite the risk, we all long to be connected to others at a heart level. All you have to do is look at the reality TV phenomenon. People put their hearts on the line in front of millions of people for the remote chance of finding love. They are inappropriately and unintelligently vulnerable because they have confused physical chemistry (connection) with committed love. The problem is that they have yet to realize the kind of relationship that they long for is developed over time and through shared experiences.

If your motivation is to find a shortcut to deeper, more intimate relationships, and if you have unrealistic expectations and are selfishly looking for the happiness you deserve, you may never find what you are looking for. You might find pleasure for a time, but you won't find joy for a lifetime.

However, if you are looking for friendships in which you connect at the heart and both can be truly yourself, then you have begun to catch the vision for the kind of relationships God desires for us.

There has got to be a better way to do this. There has got to be a way in which emotional vulnerability leads us into the kind of relationships we deeply desire.

Well, we're going to give it a shot. I'm sure you will be glad to know that many of us already possess some of the skills required to practice Intelligent Vulnerability. This book is intended to nurture the growth of these skills in you by teaching and guiding you through one process that has worked for me. As we move forward, you'll find that while many of the ways we naturally relate to one another are not healthy, we can make the necessary changes. Some are relatively easy such as changing one's perspective. Others are more difficult and require changing the way we think, like thinking positive thoughts about oneself rather than negative thoughts. Some changes happen quickly while others may take much longer.

Keep reading and you will at least be a little better prepared to develop these kinds of relationships in the future. We will do this by teaching you how to be appropriately, Intelligently Vulnerable.

Key Concepts

We don't "naturally" know how to build relationships in which we are completely loved and accepted.

Our emotional vulnerabilities, those deepest emotions, reside in our hearts.

We must protect ourselves, so we build walls around our hearts.

The desire for connection plus Emotional Vulnerability, when handled inappropriately, often leads to pain which causes us to add blocks to our walls.

Discussion Points (Group)

Should our lives be an open book to everyone? Those closest to us? As Christians?

Do you think many people feel lonely and maybe isolated?

What experiences cause us to add blocks to our walls?

Do most people desire deeper and more meaningful connections with others? Is this a realistic desire?

Getting Personal (Just for you)

Are you afraid to let others see who you really are?

Do you feel lonely and isolated?

What personal experiences have made you add blocks to your wall?

What size is your wall?

Intelligent Vulnerability: Gate to the Heart

Do you desire deeper and more meaningful connections with others? Do you believe this desire is realistic?

4
Motives for Emotional Vulnerability

It is no doubt a risky thing to open up your heart to someone. It requires opening yourself up to potential damage. Remember, that's the definition of the word vulnerable. So, what would motivate people to allow somebody behind their walls and into their hearts?

We will first look at some of the negative reasons. We have learned that we were created for intimate relationships, but our sin has interfered with the natural process. It is natural to want to open our hearts and share with those around us. The problem is, when left to our own means we sometimes find ourselves inviting people inside for selfish reasons. Selfishness is the M.O. (method of operation) of the spin-self. Let's look at some of the most common ways this occurs.

Negative Motives
Selfishness
They really don't care about the other person. They are only concerned with having their needs met, or doing what they want

to do. They don't like doing things for others unless it benefits them. It's that me-first, selfish attitude that is so prevalent in our society. It's why many people are choosing to cohabitate rather than get married. The underlying idea, even though it's not overtly stated, is, "I will be here as long as you are meeting my needs" and, "If you stop meeting my needs and making me happy, then I'm on to find somebody else who will."

Married couples can also fall into this trap. We call it adultery, and it's just another way our selfishness rears its ugly head. The simplified thought process goes something like this: "I have a need that my spouse is not meeting, and this person over there sees my need and is willing to fulfill it." They convince themselves they deserve to be happy, and happiness becomes more important than their integrity, marriage, kids, or other responsibilities in life.

Manipulation

Our old friend, the spin-self tells us, "If we don't manipulate things to get our own needs met, then we will go unfulfilled." Manipulators have come up with all kinds of ways to get what they want. Their primary desire is to get their way and control those around them. They are generally dishonest people and are willing to do whatever they can to accomplish their goals. They will use anything to get what they want, so sharing vulnerabilities just gives them more ability to manipulate. This is obviously an unhealthy way to live and will not create any healthy, intimate relationships.

Control

This is like manipulation, but the internal motives are different. The spin-self tells them they won't be happy if they are not in control. We all need a certain level of control because it ensures a level of predictably in our lives, but some people take it too far. Many times, insecurity or even anxiety causes people to take it to the extreme. Their insecurities might push them to try to act superior towards others. Other people might feel that things won't get done correctly unless it's done their way. Therefore, they feel the need to control everyone and everything in their lives. There are many different reasons people might become overly controlling but whatever the reason these people are not safe Intelligent Vulnerability partners.

Complete Me

These people are looking for somebody to complete them. I know this is such a romantic notion to many. Every time I hear somebody say this, I'm reminded of a scene in the movie, Jerry McGuire. You may know the one I'm talking about, when the couple in the elevator sign "you complete me." I must admit it is a romantic notion and makes for quite the "magical moment" on the movie screen, but it loses all its validity in the real world. In the real world, it would read "you come alongside me and enrich my life."

You see, the relationships that last are the ones where each person has a complete identity first. I believe that finding our identity in Christ is the best option, but we all know unbelievers who have great marriages too. I would suggest one common denominator is each person brings into the relationship a healthy identity and neither person is expecting or demanding of the other to make them feel complete. When we have this, other things can begin to fall into place. This person is ready to meet the other's needs first, as opposed to demanding his or her needs be met. This is a healthier relationship where people still meet each other's physical and emotional needs, which is very different from looking for someone to complete their identity.

All these negative motives will most likely leave us heartbroken resulting in building bigger walls. When we do things for these reasons, we will not get what we desire and were created for, which is true intimate relationships.

Positive reasons for emotional vulnerability

We will look at four positive reasons why we invite people behind our walls and into our hearts.

The first one trumps them all: God tells us we need them. We have already learned that God created us as social beings and intends for us to have meaningful, intimate relationships. He has placed in us a need to know those closest to us and to be known by them. He didn't put these needs in us without also giving us the ability to have them met. Sure, it came naturally and easily before the fall, but we can still have deeper, more intimate relationships today! It just takes more time and effort now.

Second, we are looking for relationships in which people come alongside us so we can walk through life together. We all desire relationships where we are confident that the person will be there for us through it all. We even put this in our standard marriage vows. We don't make formal vows to our closest friends but there is an unspoken understanding of this type of commitment. Or at least there needs to be, if we plan to be emotionally vulnerable with them.

Third, we are looking for relationships in which we both can connect at the heart level, where we connect in a place that we each feel comfortable to be ourselves.

Fourth, we desire relationships in which both people put the needs of the other before our own. It's been said that when both people are looking to meet the other's needs first, then both person's needs get met. Now this reason is primarily for the married couple since they are sharing their lives together daily.

If we put these four positive motivations together then we will have begun to catch the vision for the kind of relationships God desires for us.

As we continue, we will see how God intends to use our closest relationships both to meet our needs and, maybe just as importantly, to shape us more into His likeness. It is amid our Intelligently Vulnerable relationships that He will help us find the freedom to be who we are. We can find healing for some of our deepest vulnerabilities as we are loved and accepted, despite our flaws. And maybe, just maybe, we will begin to be able to see ourselves through the eyes of our loving Heavenly Father.

Often, this process is more than we can deal with by ourselves. Though I was a licensed professional counselor, I recognize that not everyone needs professional help. Sometimes, all we really need is a close friend and a willingness to invite him or her behind our emotional walls. The spin-self will try to tell us that we can make it on our own, that we can handle it, and that there is no need to involve anyone else. We try, often discovering that we are only lying to ourselves. But we must find a way to deal with those vulnerabilities that keep us from being free to be our best selves.

It is no doubt a risky thing to open your heart up to someone, for you might get hurt. So, what would motivate a person to allow somebody behind their wall and into their heart?

Before we move on let me ask...what do you think so far about this concept of emotional vulnerability? It's a simple concept that requires opening one's heart to another. But as we have already seen, this simple concept gets rather complicated, quickly. It's here that the road divides. Emotional vulnerability can be either intelligent or unintelligent. We just finished talking about how unintelligent vulnerability leads to more wall building in the previous chapter. Now we're going to talk about how we can make emotional vulnerability a positive experience.

Let's look again at these walls we built. Most of us have become experts at constructing walls around our hearts, haven't we? I know I have! These walls are not the problem, though. Let me say that again. These walls we build are not the problem. The problem is that many of us have forgotten that any good wall must have a gate. A functioning gate is vital to one's safety and survival. Sure, our walls keep out most of those people or things that will hurt us, but our walls also keep out those people who will bring more joy and meaning to our lives. We must learn how to build well-functioning gates that will let those people in who build us up and keep those people out who tear us down. This is the essence of Intelligent Vulnerability. Intelligent Vulnerability is self-protection without isolation.

We've made references to Intelligent Vulnerability, but

we've yet to define it. So, what is it and how is it different?

Intelligent vulnerability -- a calculated invitation, which significantly reduces the risk of potential damage, for someone to come behind my wall, by way of my gate, and accept me where I am, to help me find healing to a specific emotion or experience.

This Intelligent Vulnerability is a daunting task. It requires wisdom and skills that don't come naturally to many of us. It has always amused me that for some reason we believe we should somehow naturally know how to relate and communicate well to one another. The reality is that we are a fallen people, inherently self-absorbed. We must learn how to relate to one another in thoughtful and selfless ways. Therefore, the real-life application of emotional vulnerability has become quite complicated and indeed challenging.

Taking my wheelchair to school

I would like to be emotionally transparent and share with you a little more of my story. I have purposely used the word transparent, because I have found healing here and there is very little risk involved in sharing it with you. This will also give you some more background to understand the vulnerabilities I worked through later in my life.

I continued to lose physical strength as my muscles weakened due to the muscular dystrophy. In August of 1991, I was 14 years old, and major changes were taking place in my life. Up until this time, I had been able to remain mobile enough that I didn't need my wheelchair. Sure, I was a young teenager who was very skinny and walked with a very unusual and awkward gait, but at least I was walking. That would all change as I entered the ninth grade. I was going to have to use my wheelchair at school for the very first time. I was still able to walk to and from my morning classes, and I only had to use it from lunch until the end of the day. The problem was that the cafeteria was over in the high school building, and I was having more and more trouble walking distances. I really had no choice but to begin using my wheelchair.

I never showed any worry or concern about this new change. I just took it in stride and did what I had to do. This is what I did for many years to come. I would become the rock of Gibraltar, at least outwardly, and show the world the strong and courageous young man I was. It was here that I learned how to hide behind my faith and take something so precious and true and use it to protect myself from having to confront my deepest vulnerabilities. We're all good at this, aren't we? We have learned at a young age to use anything we can, even our faith, to spin information to protect us from any perceived threat.

It wasn't long after school had begun that I began having trouble going to sleep at night. I would lay there in bed tossing and turning, unable to fall asleep. I would finally call my dad and ask him to come lay down with me. It didn't matter what time it was; he would always come to talk to me. I would lay there in bed, sometimes with tears running down my face, and my dad would put his arms around me, hold me tight, and ask me what was wrong. What could he do to help? I would always tell him, "I don't know, Dad." He would ask me, "Son, is it that you have to take your wheelchair to school?" I would tell him, "No, I don't think so Dad. If it is, I don't know it." He would tell me that he loved me and would do anything for me.

Those were amazing and comforting words, but what was more comforting was when he would tell me that God loves me and will take care of me. He would say, "Chris, the Lord is going to heal you, maybe not in your timeframe, maybe not in my timeframe, but he will heal you." As you will see in this these pages, God has healed me...emotionally, mentally, and spiritually, and I know one day he will heal me physically too, even if it's the day I walk into heaven.

My dad looks like an amazing dad in this story, and he was the greatest dad I could have asked for, but he would tell you the real star was my mom. You see, she was the nurturing one and it would have been much easier for her to come talk to me. But she knew that I needed my dad at that moment, so she encouraged him to be the one to go talk with me. I have no doubt my mom was on her knees praying the entire time my dad was with me. My mom was the true star of this story, and she was also the greatest mom I could have asked for.

For the longest time as I looked back on this period in my life, I had a hard time figuring out what was going on in my heart. I had concluded that I was just scared about all the changes that were going on and worrying about what the future might hold for me.

While I still believe there is much truth in that statement, I now feel there was something even more profound at work. I believe the Lord was calling for me to invite Him behind my wall. I believe my inability to fall asleep was an indicator that the way I was coping wasn't working. God didn't want me to use his words as a shield to protect myself from my vulnerabilities; he wanted me to open my heart and let his words bring healing to those vulnerabilities. I hope you can see the subtle yet profound difference here. We will unpack this idea as we go along.

With this understanding, I will continue my story. I don't remember exactly how long I had difficulty falling asleep, but I'm pretty sure after a couple of weeks I had gotten over it. I continued to move forward in my life and pushed on toward my goals. I continued to get good grades in school, although they would have certainly been better if I had not been such a sociable person. I have always been outgoing and was blessed with a bunch of wonderful friends. I can't even begin to count how many piggyback rides I have been given over the years, but I think it would be safe to say it would cover hundreds of miles.

I remember one time, when my little brother was about 12, someone asked him if it was hard giving me piggyback rides. He very simply replied, "He's not heavy, he's my brother." My friends were always there for me physically, and I was there for them emotionally. I have always been the person whom my friends looked to when they needed to talk about something. It was my way of giving back to them for all the help that they had given me. We all have God-given gifts; encouraging and building relationships have been my gifts for as long as I can remember.

Closing thought

Remember back in Chapter 1 when I said I would venture to guess that very few of us have the courage to let those around us know us? I mean *truly* know us. In fact, along with the reality that we are scared to share deeply, many of us don't truly know ourselves, so how can we let others know us? Well, now it's time to look inside our own hearts to see what is inside.

Key Concepts

We must assess our motives for being emotionally vulnerable.

The walls around our hearts are not the problem. Remember, we are commanded to guard our hearts.

The problem is that any good wall requires a functioning gate that keeps out those people who will hurt us but allows in those people who will bring joy and meaning.

Intelligent vulnerability -- a calculated invitation, which significantly reduces the risk of potential damage, for someone to come behind my wall, by way of my gate, and accept me where I am, to help me find healing to a specific emotion or experience.

Discussion Points (Group)

What are some positive motives for emotional vulnerability?

What are some negative motives for emotional vulnerability?

What do you think so far about this concept of emotional vulnerability?

Do you like the concept of a functioning gate?

Do you think Intelligent Vulnerability is possible?

Getting Personal (Just for you)

What are your personal motives when you are emotionally vulnerable? Are they positive or negative? Be specific

Do you use your faith to hide from your painful vulnerabilities rather than experiencing them and working through them?

How is your gate functioning? Is it rusted shut? Is it broken? Is it missing the lock?

Are you willing to consider learning how to be Intelligently Vulnerable?

Section 2

The Process of Intelligent Vulnerability

5
Recognizing Our Vulnerabilities

We will do a quick recap before moving to the next phase of Intelligent Vulnerability. In Chapter 1, we learned the difference between emotional transparency and emotional vulnerability. In Chapter 2, we saw from Scripture that God created us for intimate relationships, but sin entered, resulting in trust being broken, and relationships now requiring work and risk. Our spin-self works to protect us by spinning information and building a wall around our hearts. In Chapter 3, we observed that our vulnerabilities, those deepest emotions, reside in our hearts. In Chapter 4, we found out the walls we build around our hearts aren't the problem, but rather the problem is that we don't have functioning gates.

These four chapters have laid the foundation for what I call Intelligent Vulnerability. We will now begin actively engaging in the process of being Intelligently Vulnerable, beginning with oneself and then sharing with those closest to us. You will notice in this section that I will begin speaking directly to you because you are the one who must choose whether to engage in the Intelligent Vulnerability process.

College

I graduated from high school in the spring of 1995 and went to college that fall. I absolutely loved my time at Ouachita Baptist University. I pledged to join the Beta Beta social club my freshman year. A social club is basically a fraternity that is not national and doesn't have a house. I loved my four years at OBU. I made many amazing friends, dated some wonderful women, and even went to class.

I graduated in four years with a Major in Christian Counseling and a Minor in Psychology. I knew that my undergraduate degree in Christian Counseling had limited use unless I continued on to get my master's degree. I looked around and quickly settled on Denver Seminary as the place I felt God calling me to continue my education. It was 1000 miles from home, but my best friend since junior high, Tony, told me that he would take a semester off from college to come up there with me and help me get settled. Tony is like a brother to me and is still one of my closest friends, a friend whom I can be Intelligently Vulnerable with. Once I was accepted, we began making plans for this move. While my parents were worried about me moving so far from home, they had raised me to be an independent young man who wasn't afraid to follow his dreams. They simply supported me and told me that they would always do everything in their power to help me achieve my goals.

Move to Denver

The time finally arrived for me to begin my journey to graduate school at Denver Seminary. My family and friends helped me load much of my belongings into a U-Haul that my dad would drive the next day. My mother and I would follow behind him in my little white minivan. We woke up early the next morning so that we could get an early start on the 15-hour drive.

This was when some of my vulnerabilities began surfacing. I very vividly remember one moment, right before I left. I was sitting inside my minivan and had just said goodbye to my little brother, and I began to feel an avalanche of emotion bubbling up inside of me. There was no way that I was going to allow myself to cry because I was getting ready to embark on the journey of a lifetime. But at that moment, I was overwhelmed by feelings of fear and excitement. I quickly regained my composure so that no one would notice my vulnerability. I mean, I had an image to uphold. The people around me saw me as a man of strength and courage. I couldn't let them see that deep down I was scared. Besides, I knew that my mom and dad were having a tough enough time letting me go to Denver as it was. So, I convinced myself that they wouldn't be able to handle me admitting to them that I was a little scared.

This was my spin-self at work trying to tell me how to act and trying to manage how others would perceive me. No doubt, my family knew of my fear, and I must admit, it was a little silly for me to think that my parents couldn't handle it. This whole issue really had nothing to do with how other people saw me, but rather with how I needed to see myself. And that was as a strong and courageous man who wasn't going to let his disability keep him from doing anything he truly wanted to do. Don't we all do this? Don't we all try to live up to this image of who we think we should be? Aren't we all afraid at some level that if people really knew us, really knew how imperfect we are, they would be disappointed? I know that I was, and I also know that this fear, at times, has kept me from truly being known by those who cared and loved me the most.

At this stage in my life, I didn't know these were signs that I had some vulnerabilities I needed to work through. So, let's look at some ways we can recognize vulnerabilities in our own lives.

Recognizing your vulnerabilities

We have laid the foundation for how we protect ourselves and why this protection is even necessary. Now we come to the place where you must decide if you want to engage in this potentially life-changing process, and if so, it begins with becoming aware of your vulnerabilities: those specific emotions or experiences deep inside your heart, the vulnerabilities your spin-self tries so desperately to hide from the world around you and often from yourself. You must be willing to courageously admit your vulnerabilities to yourself—be honest, and real with yourself. Did you already start this process in the last chapter when I asked you to list what makes up some of the blocks in your wall? Are you prepared to discover more things about yourself along the way?

It is impossible to fully share our deepest emotions if we are not aware of them. So many of us don't know our vulnerabilities because we listen to our spin-self, who either completely hides them from our inner eye or convinces us we can't handle what we find. It may be difficult and may even stretch over many months, but we can share and work through some of our deepest vulnerabilities in the context of Intelligently Vulnerable relationships.

Before we move forward in learning about the more intimate aspects of Intelligent Vulnerability, I want to make two important points. First, wait until after you have finished the book before following the suggestions concerning other people. I want you to be well prepared to engage in Intelligent Vulnerability as safely as possible. Second, you only want to confront vulnerabilities that are coming out in your life and keeping you from living healthier and better. But we must take our time because there is no timetable for healing. We will learn together how to ease ourselves into a *lifestyle* of Intelligent Vulnerability.

You might be wondering how you recognize your vulnerabilities. Let me share with you the two best ways I have found.

First, you must look at the vulnerabilities you are already acutely aware of, but also those you try to ignore or deny. One way to do this is by inward pondering. No doubt you may already know about some vulnerabilities: Childhood trauma, sickness, death, addictions, disability, divorce, abuse. There are always underlying difficult emotions that go along with these experiences.

If you find yourself afraid to talk about an experience or discover that it hurts to share it, then you most likely have a vulnerability in this area of your heart. Or if you find that you are unable to be honest about your experience or feel the need to hide it from those closest to you, then you probably have unresolved emotions you still need to work through.

We spend so much energy trying to hide these things from ourselves and the world around us. We must ask, "Why am I doing this, spending so much energy trying to fool myself and others when it's only holding me back from living a healthier life? What's the point?" The truth is most of the time we are not fooling anyone. Definitely not those who know us the best.

Have you ever taken time to sit down and take an assessment of your life? Take some time to look at your life. What might you find? Hopefully you find a lot of positives emotions and experiences but because we're fallen people, we all have negatives ones that we need to work on to become healthier and better. We must be willing to stop denying and ignoring our vulnerabilities if we are to grow and change for the better.

Here are some other questions to get you started:

Do you lack trust? Who broke that trust in your past?

Are you angry? What painful emotion are you covering up?

Were you taken advantage of? Overlooked? Betrayed?

Are you arrogant or controlling? What insecurities are you trying to cover up?

Are you bitter? What's keeping you from forgiving and letting it go? You're only hurting yourself.

Do you struggle with low self-esteem? What is keeping you from accepting yourself? Looks? Weight? Finances? Childhood scars? Intellect?

Are you rude or treat others badly so no one can hurt you?

Are you constantly negative? Maybe your excuse is 'life is unfair?'

Are you disillusioned because a hope or dream hasn't materialized?

Add your own question here if you have one.

These are difficult questions to ask ourselves. If you had the courage to search your heart, then I commend you because it's not easy. If you aren't ready yet, that's okay too. There are still more steps to learn before we can fully start practicing Intelligent Vulnerability.

Second, you can discover your vulnerabilities by simply asking those closest to you. So often we don't allow people to speak into our lives. We usually aren't open to it. Most of us don't want to know or admit our own faults to ourselves, and we sure don't want to hear about our faults from others. But this is essential if we are to truly know ourselves or those closest to us. I suggest waiting until you get a little further along in learning how to be Intelligently Vulnerable before taking this step. There are plenty of vulnerabilities you can recognize on your own first.

Diamond?

We have defined emotional vulnerability and talked generally about what some of these emotions look like, but now I want to show you what they look like through the eyes of Intelligent Vulnerability. Your vulnerabilities are diamonds! Now you may be saying to yourself "Whoa Chris, a diamond? Are you living in the same world I am? This world is full of pain and suffering. Are you really trying to tell me that all these scars, insecurities, fears, and inadequacies are precious diamonds? I don't think so!"

You may be thinking "these vulnerabilities don't seem very valuable to me, and I can assure you they are not diamonds."

You may even be saying "I can understand how my hopes and dreams may be extremely valuable, but that other stuff too? I'm not so sure." I must be very careful with this aspect of vulnerabilities. It needs to be stated clearly that some of our vulnerabilities come because of the evil and malicious actions of others, such as incest, rape, murder, and other despicable actions. If you have experienced trauma like this, I am deeply sorry you had to endure such evil. But all is not lost. There are countless stories of men and women who have found healing and then helped many others find healing. If you have experienced this depth of trauma and have not dealt with it, then I implore you to reach out to a professional counselor. Very few friends, even good ones, have the skills to help you work through your trauma.

On the other hand, I believe all of us have vulnerabilities caused by someone or something else. Let me briefly illustrate how all vulnerabilities are like a diamond. A diamond is made of pure carbon and requires tremendous pressure to form. Scientists state that it is possible for coal to turn into a diamond given the right conditions and enough time. Admittedly, some of our vulnerabilities may be more like coal but they can also be turned into diamonds when we find healing.

I suspect many of us can look back on difficult experiences we have gone through and see how the struggle has made us stronger and more resilient. Maybe someone has been through an ugly divorce, found healing, and is now able to help others experiencing something similar. Or maybe another has defeated cancer and is now able to encourage others struggling with all the fears that go with it. These are just two examples of what it means for a vulnerability to become a diamond.

We talked earlier about how our vulnerabilities reside inside our hearts. I will now ask you to consider making this more personal.

I am proposing that all emotional vulnerabilities are dispersed over three levels in your heart.

Level 1- top level filled with emotional transparencies and healed vulnerabilities.

Level 2- middle level filled with emotional vulnerabilities, some of which we are acutely aware of, and others we either ignore or deny.

Level 3- bottom level filled with emotional experiences we have forgotten or don't realize are there. This is also where deep unresolved trauma resides.

We will only venture to discuss the top 2 levels in this book. The third level, which we just briefly talked about, would almost certainly be something to be discussed with a professional counselor until you are ready to share it with a trusted friend.

On the next page, I want to encourage you to take some time and fill in some diamonds with some of your own personal transparencies or healed vulnerabilities. If you are ready, consider writing a vulnerability you've been ignoring or denying in a square. You might want to use a piece of paper for this exercise if you prefer to keep your answers private. This exercise is for your eyes only at this point, so be careful with this paper, and maybe destroy it. We haven't discussed yet how to be intelligent when sharing our vulnerabilities with others.

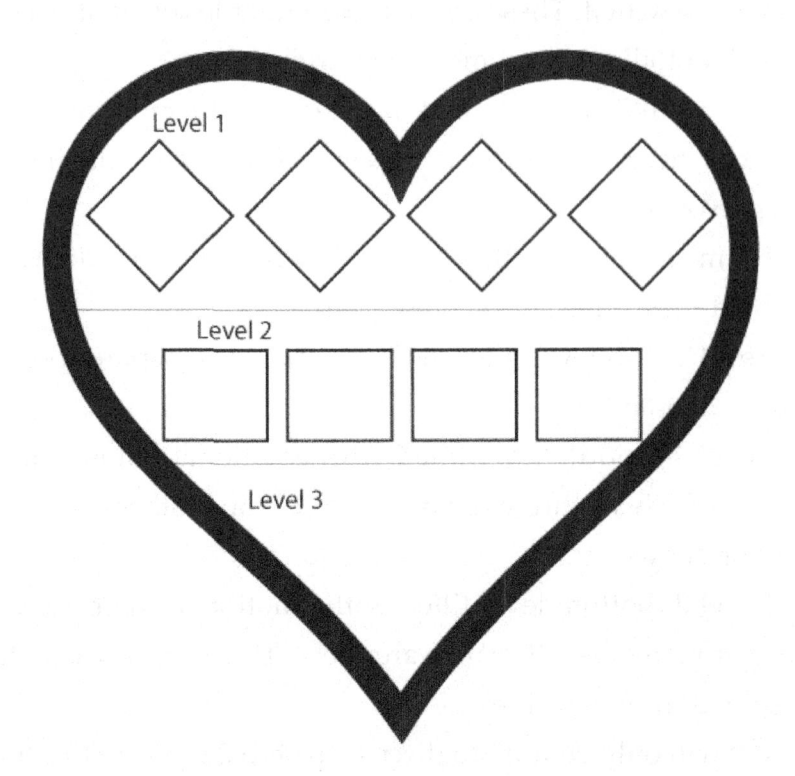

[Diagram: A heart shape containing three levels. Level 1 has four diamond shapes. Level 2 has four square shapes. Level 3 is the bottom portion of the heart.]

Supervision Group

Let me share with you one of my healed vulnerabilities, which is now a diamond, and how I finally became aware of it. When I was in graduate school, I had to take part in a supervision group as part of my counseling curriculum. This group was led by an experienced therapist, whose job was to help train us in how to be ethical professional counselors. I remember one meeting very vividly, because it involved her asking for a volunteer to role-play. I raised my hand and said that I would do it. She asked me to pick an issue that was, emotionally, a 5 on a scale of 1-10. I briefly thought about what I would pick, and quickly decided on my disability. I thought to myself, "I know this is a vulnerability, but I don't think it's a very big one for me."

She began to ask me questions about my disability, and I thought I was passing with flying colors. I don't remember all the questions specifically, but I do remember some of my answers because they were how I had been answering those questions my entire life. They were answers such as "It's hard sometimes, but God is in control" or "God has blessed me so much with amazing parents and wonderful friends. He's met my material needs and has used my disability to touch many lives, so how could I be angry or frustrated with God?" Or even, "Sure, I would much rather be walking, but if I can touch more lives for the kingdom of God in my wheelchair than I can walking, that's where I want to be." Those all sound like great, godly answers, right? Well, yes, they are!

But what came next stung me to the core. My supervisor looked me straight in the eyes and made a statement I will never forget. She said, "Chris, do you realize that you had to put a positive spin on every question I asked you?" She went on to tell me that it seemed I was unable to allow myself to feel or experience any negative thoughts, emotions, or feelings about my disability. Ouch! In five minutes, she had put her finger on a vulnerability that I thought was under control, and I must say it hurt! In fact, it took a couple of days for that pain to go away. That sting told me that my disability might be a bigger vulnerability after all. I knew that this was going to be something I would have to address at some point, but I was very unsure of how or even when to do it. The only thing I was sure of was that I had to be the one to make this decision.

It takes a lot of courage to look inside your heart and admit some of your vulnerabilities, even to yourself. Although you have now recognized some of your vulnerabilities, that doesn't mean you are ready or that you should begin dealing with them. You will see that I wasn't ready yet at this time in my life. We will look at this point in the next chapter.

Key Concepts

You must become aware of your vulnerabilities, those deep emotions or experiences in your heart, that your spin-self tries to hide both from yourself and others.

It's not yet time to share any vulnerabilities you find with another person.

You only want to confront vulnerabilities that are coming out in your life and keeping you from living healthier and better.

All your vulnerabilities are potential diamonds.

Discussion Points (Group)

What kinds of vulnerabilities do people have?

Do you think most people are aware of their vulnerabilities?

How difficult is it for people to admit their vulnerabilities to themselves?

Do you agree or disagree with our vulnerabilities being potential diamonds? Explain

Getting Personal (Just for you)

Are you willing to look at yourself and your life for vulnerabilities?

Did you take a personal assessment of your life? If not, consider doing it at some point.

Did you write down some of your vulnerabilities? If not maybe try in the future.

Do you have a past vulnerability that you would now consider a diamond?

Can you see your own vulnerabilities as potential diamonds?

6
Which Road Do I Take?

Once you have recognized a vulnerability in your heart, you should bring it before the Lord and ask for His help and healing. This deliberate act forces you to see Him as the solution rather than yourself, your best friend, or your spouse. There is no need for Intelligent Vulnerability with God because there is no risk involved. There is complete safety with the Lord because He unconditionally loves and accepts you if you have accepted Jesus as your Savior. Of course, he already knows your vulnerabilities even more than you do. He already sees the potential for your vulnerabilities to become diamonds. However, we still need to bring them before Him. No one understands like Jesus. He is the ultimate forgiver, healer, and lover of our souls.

I can remember talking to God about my vulnerabilities, but I don't think I understood clearly what emotions were buried beneath my disability. I was aware that these emotions were real, but I had convinced myself that this wasn't a vulnerability that I could adequately deal with as a single person. Looking back, I'm disappointed that I believed this and used it as an excuse. But I think that we all make excuses when we don't want to do something. I did ask the Lord to show me if this was something I needed to start working on. And boy did he ever show me.

Are you ready to continue looking within yourself? Are you ready to talk to God about your deepest emotions? Are you ready to courageously begin dealing with your vulnerabilities? Many of us have passively accepted the circumstances in our lives and have become captives of those circumstances. We have given in and given up. We forget that God created us as free beings and we are free to make our own choices. It has been said that we become what we choose to be. Who will you choose to be? Will you choose to stay stuck in the mud, spinning your wheels, listening to the lies of your spin-self? Are you unwilling to change or step out of your comfort zone? Are you afraid to hope that life could be more fulfilling and meaningful?

Or will you be the person who courageously ventures into that place where most people are unwilling to go? That place where you see yourself as you truly are and choose to confront your vulnerabilities. Where you grow towards finding healing, freedom, and more meaningful relationships.

One of my favorite stories that shows us the importance of being willing to step out of our comfort zones is that of baby eagles. They have lived safely in the nest, being cared for and fed by their parents, but they don't live in the nest forever. They must venture out and this starts by watching their parents fly. Then they begin jumping around in the nest and flapping their wings. The next thing you know, they begin taking small flights from one branch to another. The more they practice, the better they get. Eventually, the eagle becomes a proficient flier and ventures out of the only place it's ever known and discovers the freedom to experience flight. We, too, must venture out of our comfort zones if we want to experience greater freedom to be our best self and develop more intimate relationships.

So, what about you? I believe that God is asking all of us to bring our vulnerabilities before Him. He is calling us out of our comfort zones. Are you ready to look to the Lord and begin healing? I can tell you from personal experience that there is new freedom when we find healing for our vulnerabilities.

3 Roads

If you have now become aware of a specific vulnerability in your life and brought it before the Lord, then you have come to a fork in the road. You have a decision to make, and I can think of three alternatives. Road One is not a very good one but is the one we usually choose. Road Two is a better choice, but it brings no true healing or closure. Road Three is the riskiest, but in time it leads us to healing and freedom like we have never known before.

Road One isn't clearly a road so you don't realize that you need to turn left or right. Instead, you just keep going and make your own path. In this option, you decide to ignore, or deny that you have a vulnerability. We attempt to go on like nothing ever happened and the vulnerability was never exposed. Road One is bumpy for a while, but it eventually evens out. There's little growth here, but it is comfortable because it's all we have known. Most of us would rather stay in our comfort zone, in the place where we know what to expect and how to act, than venture into an unknown situation.

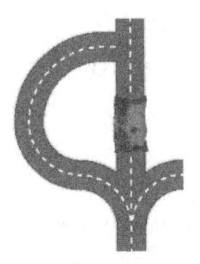

Road Two curves off to the left. There is nothing wrong with choosing to take this road. It is on this road that you admit that you have found a specific vulnerability that probably needs to be worked on, but you're not ready to confront it yet, so you avoid situations or conversations that might make you have to face it. There are many legitimate reasons to take this road, and we will address them shortly. The problem with Road Two is that the vulnerability still resides, and it will eventually take you back to where you began.

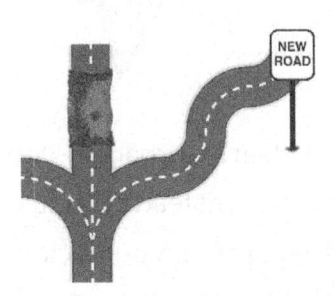

Road Three (next page) curves off to the right. This road seems scary because we don't know where it leads. In fact, it sometimes seems like Road Three takes you backward at the start. It is on Road Three that we choose to confront a specific vulnerability in our lives. We act appropriately, intelligently, and courageously while venturing into uncharted territory.

Unlike the other two roads, Road Three eventually takes us to a new road that is no longer encumbered by that old vulnerability. This book is meant to equip us with the proper knowledge so that we can safely and intelligently venture down this road.

After bringing my supervision experience before the Lord, I continued to take Road Two during the coming weeks due to my belief that these vulnerabilities weren't holding me back from becoming healthier and freer. However, I talked to some friends about it, and they all encouraged me to begin dealing with it now. I stood firm in my decision in the beginning. I had written off other people's opinions because they didn't know me as well as I knew myself. I was fooling myself. In the coming months, God would make this extremely clear, as he is accustomed to doing with me.

Only after you admit your vulnerabilities to yourself and then bring them before the Lord can healing finally begin in your heart. Once you have taken this step you are ready to consider moving forward with the Intelligent Vulnerability process.

There are two major questions to ask yourself before you decide which road to take in dealing with a specific vulnerability.

The first question is:

Does this vulnerability, and potential diamond, affect my everyday living or my interactions with those I care about most?

1. If the answer is no, it may not be worth the time, effort, or risk required to adequately work through and deal with this vulnerability.

2. If your answer is yes, then decide to what extent this vulnerability affects you.

Ken L. conversation

I can remember one conversation that occurred shortly after I had begun wrestling with whether I needed to start working through the vulnerability of my disability with my trusted friends. I had been assigned a dyad partner who happened to be my good friend Ken. When you are first training to become a counselor, they do not trust you yet to see clients, so you practice on each other, and this is called dyad partners. You counsel your partner, and then your partner counsels you. It is basically a way for you to practice the counseling skills you are learning in class, and it's also an opportunity to see what it feels like to be a client.

I remember sitting on my scooter in a conference room, one day, at the Denver Seminary library. Ken was counseling me, and I brought up that I was struggling with whether I should delve into the vulnerabilities surrounding my physical disability. I told him that I realized I had some pain, frustration, anger, and fear concerning my disability, but I didn't feel like it was hurting my interactions with others.

I also told him that I felt like I was coping well with everything and that I wasn't sure if it would be worth the risk to unpack all that was there. I was afraid that embracing my vulnerabilities and letting myself feel them might break me down and leave me broken and bitter. I can remember vividly asking Ken, "If I go down this road, can you promise me that I will be better for it?"

He responded very astutely that he would walk down that road with me, but that there was no way he could guarantee what the result would be. I appreciated his honesty and chose at that time not to go down that road yet, because I wasn't ready to engage in the process and take full responsibility for the outcome. It was unrealistic and unfair of me to ask Ken to give me a guarantee that it would be worth the risk. After all, he is not God, and he does not know the future.

That was a choice and risk I needed to decide whether to take or not. In the same way, you too must be the one to take responsibility for engaging in the Intelligent Vulnerability process. This process of facing vulnerabilities must begin within one's own heart. It cannot be forced on anybody. Each person must make his or her own choice to confront his or her vulnerabilities.

This leads us to the second question.

Does the potential reward outweigh the potential risk involved?

1. If the answer is no, you may want to wait until you are confident it's worth the risk to work through this vulnerability.

2. If the answer is yes, you must be ready to take full responsibility for your role in working through this vulnerability.

At that time, I answered "no" to this question. I wasn't ready to admit that it was something I needed to work on, and I didn't believe the risk was worth the reward.

It was time

About this time, I lost a significant amount of strength in my left shoulder. This loss of strength meant that it was no longer possible for me to drive my minivan and it also meant that I would now have much more trouble feeding myself from a table. I would now need somebody to hand me my fork and I would only be able to eat things that I could stab with a fork. I had faced adversity in my life many times before but for some reason this time it was different. It was different because I was in one of the most amazing and challenging periods of personal growth that I have ever experienced.

I remember one meal very vividly. My brother, Robbie, and his wife, Betsy, had invited me and our parents to have lunch with them. Betsy had cooked a pot roast along with mashed potatoes and creamed corn. I was having trouble feeding myself and after my dad was done eating, he came over and sat down next to me, took my fork from me, and helped me finish my plate. My friends, let me tell you, this was one of the hardest and most humbling things I have ever experienced. I remember thinking "I can't believe that I need somebody to help feed me!"

I knew that the time had come for me to start actively working through my vulnerabilities surrounding my disability. I was ready to take on full responsibility for working through these emotions. This was an extremely difficult task for me because I had never allowed myself to question God. My faith in God was where I found the strength and courage to make the best out of my situation in life. Trusting that God was in control and had a plan for my life gave me hope and a purpose. I had also stood on the belief that God was good and only wanted what was best for me. I told myself and was told by others that God was using my wheelchair to touch the lives of those around me for his kingdom.

Ultimately, I believed that God was in control and working things for my good and his glory. So how could I question God, or worse yet, how could I be angry with him? Would feeling these negative emotions be a sign of weakness and a lack of faith and trust in God? I can remember struggling with this very issue. I felt that giving in to any of these negative emotions would mean that I was allowing my disability to defeat me.

You see, I had taken a great deal of pride in how I had handled my disability up to this point. It was my pride. At some level, I took pride in the fact that I had accomplished so much in life despite my disability. There was no way I was going to allow anybody to see how vulnerable I really was in this area. Weakness and defeat were just not words that were in my vocabulary. So, I had to ask myself a very important question: Would confronting these negative emotions be a sign of weakness and defeat or would it be another sign of strength and courage? Would they be a sign of lack of faith or rather a sign of trusting God in faith?

The answer was loud and clear: It was time to take Road Three. I realized the ability and willingness to confront one's deepest pains and vulnerabilities takes an enormous amount of strength and courage. In fact, it takes the kind of courage that very few people can muster on their own. It also takes the help of some extremely special people to love and protect you as you venture into this scary and unknown territory. It is vital that the people with whom you share this deep vulnerability treat this area with the utmost care. This vulnerability is like a diamond that must be seen as precious and handled carefully. It is so valuable that to attack this area could crush the spirit and cause deeper wounds.

This is where and why Intelligent Vulnerability is vital to developing intimate relationships! Now that you have admitted your vulnerabilities to yourself and to God, it's time to consider which road to travel. Will it be Road Two or Road Three? Remember, Intelligent Vulnerability will tell you which road to take.

My tears

My journey on Road Three continued one evening when I was finally able to get honest with myself before God. I was lying on my couch talking to God about my physical disability and all the emotions that went with it. For the first time in my life, tears began to roll down my cheeks specifically because of the physical loss I had experienced. I finally allowed myself to ask that question WHY? I allowed myself to feel some anger about my situation. To grieve my losses. To feel disappointment. I was no longer hiding my disability behind my faith or coming up with other excuses to avoid feeling and beginning to work through those negative emotions stored in my heart. This was a cathartic experience for me, and I knew that healing had begun. The foundation had been laid, and now I was ready to begin engaging in Intelligent Vulnerability to continue the healing process.

Faith as a shield

As we close this chapter, I want to briefly address the fact that many of you reading this book may not be professing Christians. In fact, some might be atheists. Most atheists believe that religion is nothing more than a psychological crutch for the weak-minded to help them avoid reality. Karl Marx said, "Religion is the impotence of the human mind to deal with occurrences it cannot understand." They often believe it's the greatest form of escaping what they believe to be true, that ultimately life is futile because if there is no God then there is no afterlife and life has no purpose beyond self-fulfillment.

I readily admit that up until this time in my life, I had been using my faith as a shield, not just as protection from the devil, as the Bible tells us in Ephesians 6:16, but as a shield to hide behind so I could avoid dealing with my deepest vulnerabilities or emotions. I didn't do this because I was weak-minded or to protect myself from the reality that my life was meaningless. On the contrary, I was protecting the vulnerabilities in my heart, those painful emotions surrounding my disability that I was not ready to confront. Despite this fact, there was no question that my faith was genuine and my salvation secure. I just needed to continue growing and maturing in my walk with Jesus.

I was recently talking with a man in my church, and he stated he often hears people say all the right things and quote the right Scriptures, but it was different with me because he felt I genuinely believed it. He then asked how I got to the point where I was truly content in my life despite being confined to a power wheelchair and needing help with almost everything. The short answer is: Christ and Christ alone. He has given me the gift of faith. Faith to trust that His Word is true and faith that I can build my identity in Him. But the Lord didn't just miraculously make me content. It was a process that required time in the Bible, prayer, worship, and Intelligently Vulnerable relationships. I will share some of the stories of this healing in the coming chapters. You will see that I found healing, and the words of Scripture were no longer an external shield but had become an internal truth. If you will let God's truth into your heart, then he will begin transforming and healing your vulnerabilities. Will you have the courage to engage in Intelligently Vulnerable relationships and let God transform you through them?

Key Concepts

There is complete safety in bringing our vulnerabilities before the Lord.

We must step out of our comfort zones if we want to find healing, freedom, and more intimate relationships.

Three Roads after you've become aware of a vulnerability

Road One - Here you decide to try to forget, ignore, and deny that this is a vulnerability.

Road Two – Here, you admit that you have found a vulnerability that needs to be worked on, but you're not ready to confront it yet.

Road Three - It is on this road that you choose to confront a vulnerability.

Two questions to help determine which road to take.

Does this vulnerability, and potential diamond, affect my everyday living or my interactions with those I care about most?

1. If not, it may not be worth the time, effort, or risk required to adequately work through and deal with this vulnerability.

2. If yes, then decide to what extent this vulnerability affects you.

Does the potential reward outweigh the potential risks involved?

1. If the answer is no, you may want to wait until you are

confident it's worth the risk to work through this vulnerability.

2. If yes, then you must be ready to take full responsibility for your role in working through this vulnerability.

One's faith should be used as a shield against the devil, Ephesians 6:16. But it shouldn't be used to hide behind so one can avoid dealing with one's vulnerabilities.

Discussion Points (Group)

Is it important to bring your vulnerabilities before the Lord?

Have you just accepted your circumstances or believe that your situation can't be changed? Do you feel stuck?

Do you agree or disagree that we largely become who we choose to be?

What does it look like to step out of your comfort zone?

Is allowing yourself to experience negative emotions like pain or grief a sign of weakness? Strength? Lack of faith? Faith to trust God?

Do you understand how to determine whether you're ready to start working on a specific vulnerability?

What is the difference between using faith as protection from the devil and using it to hide behind to avoid dealing with a vulnerability?

Getting Personal (Just for you)

Who do you want to be?

What choices must you make to begin working towards that goal or becoming that person?

Is there something specific you could do to step out of your comfort zone?

Could you take some small steps to get out of your comfort zone?

Are you ready to allow yourself to begin working through some of your painful emotions? Remember, it's okay and maybe even right if you're not ready yet.

Is there a specific vulnerability you are ready to admit to yourself and God? If so, which road will you choose? Road Two or Road Three?

Are you using your faith to hide behind so you can avoid dealing with a vulnerability in your life?

7
Confronting Our Vulnerabilities

You must learn to recognize your vulnerabilities, bring them before the Lord, and be ready to take full responsibility for your role in working through the emotions. Once you have done these three things, you are ready to move on to the next step in the Intelligent Vulnerability process. It is here that you begin confronting your vulnerabilities whenever you see them in your life.

Craig Hospital -- Summer internship

I frequently conversed with God and continued to take small steps towards coming to grips with my vulnerabilities surrounding my disability. I was slowly working towards resolutions and thought I was doing a pretty good job on the matter. However, I quickly found out that I had only just begun a tough, yet extremely rewarding journey.

As my fourth semester ended, I began looking for a summer internship in the counseling field so that I could begin accumulating counseling hours toward graduation.

I met with my internship coordinator, and she encouraged me to look at a possible internship at Craig Hospital. This is a world-renowned brain and spinal cord injury hospital. My first response was thinking, "Absolutely not!"

I had no desire to work with people in similar conditions to myself. I didn't want to be confronted with my own disability on a regular basis. Remember, I had not viewed myself as disabled. Sure, all the patients at Craig Hospital were disabled, but for some reason, I didn't think I was like them. The idea of working there was uncomfortable to me. I think that deep down I knew they were no different than me, and I wasn't ready to admit it.

Although God never spoke audibly to me, I was certain that he was calling me there as much as I didn't want to work there. You see, I believe that God often confirms his will to us through our family, friends, mentors, spiritual leaders, and others.

It didn't matter who I talked to; everybody encouraged me to take this internship and told me that I would be wonderful at it. I remember wishing that just one person would tell me not to take it, but that one person never came. I finally decided, after much struggle, that it would be foolish of me not to listen to those around me.

I took the internship and became a chaplain/counseling intern at Craig Hospital. It turned into an amazing experience for me because I needed to step out of my comfort zone and actively begin confronting my vulnerability for healing to continue. After all, there were at two ways to look at this.

Two primary ways to confront your vulnerabilities

The first primary way to confront your vulnerabilities is to start looking for situations or events that force you to work on your specific vulnerability. The story above illustrates this one.

We will deal with the first way here, but there is no specific way this must be done. It could be as simple as singing karaoke when you are afraid of being up in front of groups. It could be going to church when you haven't been in months because you know you haven't been living right. Maybe you go out to dinner alone when you worry about what people think about you. We can come up with all kinds of ideas to confront a specific vulnerability. If you have taken responsibility for working through a specific emotion or experience, then you will inherently know some things you can do to actively confront it. Other times, life will naturally put opportunities in your path. You just must be courageous enough to step out of your comfort zone and take advantage of the opportunities when they come.

Are you ready to take this vital step toward confronting your vulnerabilities and mining your diamonds?

We would be wise to take this vital step toward finding our healing and freedom and stop avoiding it. It's time to realize that our excuses are hindering us from living more fully. We can no longer let our fear of failure keep us frozen in place. We must look our pride in the face and no longer let it hold us captive. We must venture out of our comfort zone, thereby overcoming that fear of the unknown. Our excuses to avoid confronting our vulnerabilities, as legitimate as some might be, do nothing to bring us the healing and relationships we so desire.

Let me encourage you for a second. If you have made it this far, then you are stronger and more courageous than maybe you give yourself credit for. The reality is that most people don't realize the benefits of confronting their vulnerabilities or they are too afraid of what they might find.

Let me talk with you a little more about physical disability. In a world that is focused on physical appearance, people look at my situation and tend to feel sorry for me or think that I've got it hard. Sure, it's not easy having to ask people for help with the simplest things, but let's get past the superficial façade that we all live in. We all are often preoccupied with things that we can see with our eyes, things like physical beauty and strength. Therefore, we look at a person with a physical disability and are immediately cognizant of their physical limitations. Often the next response is something like "I sure am glad that's not me" or maybe "I wonder if I would be able to handle life if I were in that situation." These are all normal reactions that people have, and they are not something that one should be ashamed of thinking. Let me encourage you now to ask yourself these questions. Pause here and take some time to think about how you would deal with life if you had some kind of physical disability. Could you handle it? Would you make the best of it and overcome it? Or would you give up and be miserable?

What did you come up with? Are you confident in your answer? I believe I can tell you an easy way to be confident about how you would respond. You see, people tend to make a physical disability seem like a bigger obstacle than it really is. It's an outgrowth of the society that we live in. Here is the reality: we are all disabled. Every person on this earth has some sort of disability. It may not be evident to the world like mine is, but it is there.

Some of you reading this book may have been physically, emotionally, or sexually abused as a child or even as an adult. Others may have serious issues concerning anger management or major self-esteem issues. Others may not be able to trust anybody because they have been hurt so many times. Maybe you struggle with depression, anxiety, or some other mental illness. The list can go on and on. I wonder what it would be like if just for a day we had glasses that allowed us to see the emotional or mental scars that people carry with them each and every day. I bet that if we could do this, a physical disability would become much less of a focus. In fact, I believe we would begin to see that a physical disability, as hard as it may be, is not the hardest thing that people must deal with. It's just the one that is most obvious. So, how would you deal with a physical disability?

I would venture to guess that you would deal with it the same way that you deal with other issues in your life. Many people have said to me, "Chris, I don't know how you do it. I'm not sure I would be able to handle it as well as you do." They may not think they would respond so positively, but I know better. The human spirit is an amazingly resilient and courageous thing.

I learned this first-hand at my Craig Hospital internship. The ones who make it through the big trials are the same ones who never give in to the little ones. You'll never win the war if you don't fight the battles. We all fight battles every day, some big and some small. Some we win, and some we lose, but those who keep fighting allow themselves the chance for a victorious life.

The second primary way to confront your vulnerabilities is to ask the people closest to you how your specific vulnerability affects them or your relationship.

This is just as straightforward as it sounds. The ideal person would be someone who understands the Intelligent Vulnerability process and knows how sensitive this vulnerability is to you. Obviously, that's not always possible so use the knowledge you've learned in this book and assess whether they are a safe person to open your heart to.

This step takes even more courage; because there is much more risk involved. I have placed it here because it is a part of confronting a vulnerability, but I would suggest waiting until later in your Intelligent Vulnerability journey before tackling this one. You will see in my next story that I didn't begin directly asking my closest friends how my disability had affected our relationship until I was well down the road in my Intelligent Vulnerability journey.

Difficult talk with Ken W.

I desired to know the truth about how my disability affected not only me but also those around me. I can remember, towards the end of the process, after God had already done much healing on my heart, finally being ready to honestly hear how my disability affected others. I was not so interested in the positive side of this question because I had often heard those answers before, but I had never had the courage to look directly into the negative side.

One conversation sticks with me today because of the

straight and honest answer that my good friend told me. When I was living in Denver, during my last semester in seminary, I lost my caregiver who had been helping me get showered and dressed in the mornings. One of my good friends said that he would be happy to do it because he needed some extra money anyway. This turned out to be a good situation for the most part and worked well for my remaining time in Denver. When I began looking back on that time, I realized one big difference that had occurred.

Some months after I had moved back to Arkansas, to be close to my family, I called Ken up and asked him about this change. He understood I had been working on coming to grips with my disability and knew that I was looking for the truth. He began sharing with me that once he began as my caregiver, things began to change for him. You see, we used to hang out more on the weekends, but he told me that he began finding that he needed a break from helping me. I must admit that these words hurt as he shared them, but they were exactly what I needed to hear.

This conversation gave me insight into my life as a disabled person. It was primarily this conversation that changed my mind about what I was looking for in my future wife. I had fooled myself into thinking that most of my needs were things that some women desire to do for their husbands anyway, so I was looking for a wife who had that caregiving nature. I had been looking for a wife who would help me hide from my disability and pretend like it didn't matter. The cold, hard truth is that I do have a physical disability and it does matter.

It was here that I decided I could no longer hide from my

disability, but that I must embrace it. It meant that I made the decision that I would now look for a woman to be my wife and not my wife/caregiver. The reality is that it is impossible to be a part of my life without sometimes helping me with things, but I decided that whatever woman God chose for me would not have to feel the burden of being my primary caregiver. This would have a profound effect on my life because if I had not grown in this area, then I would not be married to my beautiful and amazing wife, Lisa, today. Nor would I be blessed with my two incredible children, Caitlan and Ayden. So, my willingness to be Intelligently Vulnerable not only brought me great insight and healing into my life but also directly led to the fulfillment of my dream of getting married and having a family. This change came because I used my gate properly and let the right people behind my wall and into my heart. The fact that I let in people who brought about positive change in my life tells me I used my gate well.

So why wait?

Some of you may be sitting here thinking that all this stuff is great for other people, but not for you. You are convinced that for some reason you are not strong enough or courageous enough to admit your vulnerabilities to yourself, or better yet risk sharing those vulnerabilities with someone close to you and letting them know you and love you. You sit unfulfilled in your comfort zone instead of experiencing the healing and intimate relationships that your heart may be longing for. Maybe you've read up to this point in the book without applying any of it to your own life. If this is you, then just know there is nothing to be ashamed of. You may not be ready yet. The great thing is that it will be here when you are ready. It's never too late to work on becoming a healthier and freer person.

Many of us never venture out of this comfort zone until a crisis strikes. I find it sad that it usually takes a crisis before people are willing to reach out and be vulnerable with one another. But isn't this true? How many times have you been involved in or heard stories about how people come together in times of crisis? So many times, we only reevaluate our life and what is truly important when we are confronted with losing someone or something. I believe that it is in these times that our true strength comes out. Why is it that we must be faced with a crisis before we are willing to be truly vulnerable and allow someone to completely love and care for us? There is no reason to wait for a crisis in your life before you step out of your comfort zone and into Intelligently Vulnerable relationships.

After you have admitted a vulnerability to yourself, shared it with God, taken responsibility for its resolution, and have begun actively confronting it, then true healing has begun. It is at this point that you begin contemplating inviting those closest to you behind your wall and into your heart. It is here that we must assess our motives for emotional vulnerability before we can move forward with Intelligent Vulnerability.

Key Concepts

Two primary ways you can confront your vulnerabilities:

The first primary way is to look for situations or events that force you to work on your specific vulnerability.

The second primary way is to ask the people closest to you how a specific vulnerability of yours affects them or your relationship.

Asking others about your vulnerability is best used later in the Intelligent Vulnerability process after substantial healing has already occurred.

Discussion Points (Group)

Give some ideas of situations that someone could use to confront a specific vulnerability?

What excuses do people use to avoid confronting their vulnerabilities? Are any legitimate?

If you could wear glasses that allowed you to see people's vulnerabilities, would it change anything? Maybe how you see yourself? Would you be more patient? Show more grace?

What happens to people's connection with others after a crisis or tragedy?

Getting Personal (Just for you)

Do you make excuses to avoid confronting a specific vulnerability?

Is there a situation you could put yourself in to help you

confront a specific vulnerability? Are you ready to try?

When life gets difficult or unfair, do you find ways to overcome it, or do you give up?

Have you experienced a deeper level of connection with others during a crisis or tragedy? Did it change you? Did it last?

8
Are You Ready? Three Big Questions

We will begin to transition from being vulnerable with oneself to being vulnerable with another person. But before we move on to the next phase of Intelligent Vulnerability, we must look at three more important questions regarding our motives.

Three big questions

First big question: Are my motives for sharing my vulnerabilities with those I care about most, positive or negative?

In this first question, we will look at some negative motives for emotional vulnerability. Then, in the next two questions, we will address positive motives.

Although emotional vulnerability can have profoundly wonderful benefits, we can still abuse and cheat this exchange. Sometimes people are so overwhelmed with feelings of guilt or embarrassment that they disclose their situation to someone solely to relieve their own troubled spirit without thought of the burden placed on that person. This kind of negative vulnerability is selfish and does more harm to the relationship than it does good. What this person is doing is using vulnerability as a tool to meet his or her own needs. Living one's life with a me-first attitude will always have a negative impact on our relationships.

Some people choose to use vulnerability to play the "poor me" card. This is just an attempt to manipulate those around them. These people expect special treatment because of their struggles or scars. They use their vulnerability as an excuse to continue living in the same rut. They may desire to change but can never seem to do what it takes to make the hard choices required to find the healing they desire. So, they live defeated lives because they cannot seem to break free from that old vulnerability. Life is hard because it appears that they do not like themselves very much and are constantly looking for acceptance and approval from those around them. Sadly, their actions often keep them from the relationships they desire.

Others use vulnerability to unload their emotional baggage on others. This often includes sharing much too deeply, and/or too quickly. It is not genuine vulnerability, but rather it is another way to attempt to manipulate and control those around them into being an ally or to gain sympathy. We all know people who will tell anyone all their troubles just after meeting them. This is selfish and deceptive and ends up being detrimental to all involved. All it accomplishes is scaring off people who might otherwise be a friend, leaving the sharer feeling ashamed and alone.

Another misuse of vulnerability is when people continually share with the wrong people. Their overwhelming need for intimacy overpowers common sense. They are so desperate to be loved that they lay their hearts on the line with anyone who shows the smallest amount of interest. This is unhealthy and does not lead to lasting, healthy relationships.

The quickest way to destroy a friendship is to break the trust that has been built up over time. Betrayed trust is serious business. Trust is something many of us struggle to give out, so a betrayed trust takes a tremendous amount of time and work to rebuild. And many times, once it has been broken, that trust is never recovered. Let's make sure our motives are right when we choose to be emotionally vulnerable so that we can build trust with those who are the closest to us.

Right person, wrong time

Vulnerability can also be negative if shared at the wrong time. There are times when we know we have found a certain friend or a spouse who is safe enough for us to open up our hearts. Even if we have found the right person to be vulnerable with, that doesn't mean that we can talk to them anytime we want. We need to find the best time with the least number of distractions.

This would include picking a time when you are both fully awake since it's not a good idea to engage in meaningful conversation when one or the other is sleepy. If your wife likes to wake up early in the morning, then it's not ideal to start a deep conversation late at night. Also, if your husband is a night owl, then it's not ideal to start a conversation first thing in the morning. This may seem obvious, but it is easy to forget. If we pick the wrong time to share, we are setting ourselves up for disappointment because the listener can't fully engage in the process.

Likewise, it is not a good time to share if one or both of you are exhausted after a long, hard day. When we are tired, we lose many of the qualities required to engage in healthy conversation. We find that our patience runs thin, our attention span decreases, and our capacity to be compassionate grows short. This creates a tremendous problem since we need these qualities in full force if we are to be intelligent about our vulnerability. Otherwise, the risk of being hurt or misunderstood greatly increases.

It also may not be a good time to share if one or both of you are overwhelmed and stressed out. This is a hard one because many of us might be thinking that it will never be a good time if we must wait until we're not stressed. Sadly, living our lives full of stress has become the norm, so we are unlikely to avoid it.

The key here is to not be vulnerable with someone when either of you are so overwhelmed with life that it feels like we're doing all we can just to survive. It requires substantial emotional energy to share our hearts and work through our vulnerabilities, or be the listener, so we need to be sure we are ready for the challenge.

There are certainly other factors in our lives that make it the wrong time to be vulnerable even if we have found the right person to be vulnerable with. Take just a minute to think about your life. What factors might keep you from being ready to be vulnerable? Maybe you're not ready to be Intelligently Vulnerable right now. There is nothing wrong with that. It could be you just need more time to grow like you will see in this next story.

Tiffany story

After I moved to Denver, it didn't take me long before I made a good friend who was a girl. I had been friends with a lot of girls in the past, but Tiffany was very different from the girls I usually became friends with. We had little in common except for the fact that we both enjoyed watching TV. We laugh now about how awkward our friendship was in the beginning because she would pretty much come over to watch TV and drink my cokes. I didn't mind too much though because I enjoyed her company. She was one of those girls you could talk to about any subject and that made for an interesting visit.

She would tell you that she was a pretty selfish person back then. I hated to ask her for anything, even small things like getting me a glass of juice because I felt like I was putting her out. In fact, she has told me since then that she saw my need to ask for help as weakness and that it annoyed her to have to help me with anything. She said that her view of a man was one of physical strength and independence. Therefore, my disability and the fact that I had no choice but to ask people for help, in her eyes, made me a weak person. This was a view that would change as our friendship progressed.

Tiffany and I shared dinner during the week before I moved back home. She drove out to my condo to pick me up for the night. We went to dinner downtown at a place called Cafe Brazil. It was a small little restaurant that wasn't very handicapped accessible. The waiters had to carry my wheelchair, and me, up two small stairs to get inside.

Once we got inside, the atmosphere was great. We started

off with an appetizer of calamari, which was fabulous. I had ordered this mahi-mahi covered with pineapple and all kinds of nuts. It looked wonderful but there was a problem. It was so tender that there was no way I was going to be able to use my fork to eat it on my own.

Tiffany was happy to help me with my meal, fortunately. I don't think either of us could believe what was occurring. Some people in the restaurant were looking at us, but we didn't care. We were enjoying one of the most memorable meals that we would ever share, and it was an amazing example of how much each of us had grown because of our friendship together. I chose to share this story because I think it's a great example of how people and friendships can change. I never would have guessed that a friendship that began so superficially would, in time, become one where I could be Intelligently Vulnerable.

Her helping me eat dinner illustrated incredible growth and healing in both our lives. This friendship is a good example that we should never completely rule out a certain friend from becoming an Intelligent Vulnerability partner. We can all grow and mature and become kinder, more compassionate people if we're willing to work on it.

If you have now assessed your motives and feel confident that they are not negative, then it's time to assess if you're ready to share for the right reasons. These next two big questions will help you assess if your motives are positive and whether it is time to seriously consider if you need to be Intelligently Vulnerable with others.

Second big question: Do I need to be Intelligently Vulnerable?

I have listed three statements, and you decide whether they are true or false before moving on with this process. Also listed are some examples concerning each question, but they are not exhaustive. Therefore, you may want to write your own examples concerning your specific vulnerability.

True or False—My vulnerability is negatively affecting my life or my relationships with others.
<u>Examples.</u>
1. We avoid someone or something so that our avoidance hinders our day-to-day life.
2. We have low self-esteem that keeps us from performing at our best.
3. We have issues of trust: We can't trust others, or we can't be trusted.
4. We are struggling with an addiction on our own.
5. We have problems saying "no" to people.

True or False—I spend considerable time maintaining my image.
<u>Examples</u>
1. We avoid people or situations where a weakness may be exposed.
2. We are fearful of being wrong or inadequate.
3. We are living a secret life and afraid of being found out.
4. We tend to isolate ourselves and avoid spending time with others.

True or False—I realize that I need to confront my vulnerability to move forward in my life and find freedom to be my best self.

Examples

1. The spin doesn't work anymore. We come to see that we are lying to ourselves.

2. We realize we have worked ourselves into a corner and are looking for a way out.

3. We realize that we must mimic others or identify with others to have an identity.

If you answered "false" to all three statements, then you are doing better than me because I still struggle with all three at times and may for the rest of my life. But, if you're like me and would answer true to at least parts of all three statements, then you must decide to what extent your vulnerability affects you. If you feel like the effect is minimal, then you may not feel like it is worth the time, effort, or risk required to adequately work through and deal with your vulnerability at this time.

On the other hand, if you read these three statements and feel like your vulnerabilities are holding you back from living a more genuine life, then you have three other important questions to ask. Don't just quickly read over these questions but take a minute and think about them.

1. Are you willing to make the time required to ponder and talk through your vulnerability?
2. Are you ready to put out the effort it takes to work through a specific vulnerability?

3. Are you confident the potential reward outweighs the potential risks involved?

The reality is, that Intelligent Vulnerability takes work, and working through hard and painful issues takes discipline and commitment. There's no shame in answering that you are not ready to confront your vulnerabilities at this time. In fact, I would suggest that you wait to engage in Intelligent Vulnerability with another person until you can answer all three questions with a yes.

Now if you answered yes to all three questions, then you are ready to move on to the third major question. It's the one question that personally took me the longest to answer with a yes and was the hardest for me to come to grips with. But it is necessary if we are to move forward in the Intelligent Vulnerability process.

Third big question: Are you ready to take responsibility for what and how much you share?

If you are ready to engage in the process of Intelligent Vulnerability, then you must take personal responsibility for both what you share and how much you share. In doing so, you can do some things that will help you to manage the risk. The first is to test the waters. You should begin with small increments of confidence in which we share smaller bits of information. A simple way to do this is to be transparent concerning a situation in your life that you have already worked through. Then just wait and see what this person does with this information. If by next week, everyone at work or in your Sunday school class knows what you told this person, then you can be sure you would not want to share your deeper vulnerabilities with him or her. The key is not bearing your soul before you are sure your vulnerabilities are safe with that person.

You also need to make sure the person is open to hearing what you desire to share. The reality is there are certain things that not all people can hear or are equipped to deal with. Even if the person is open to hearing, we need to have some idea of how he or she will respond to what we intend to share. We must also avoid the shock factor by preparing the listener for what we are about to share. It may be saying something like "I need to share something with you that is very vulnerable to me" or "I am struggling with something really big, and I'm going to need you to come alongside me and listen." This sort of statement will go a long way toward helping you get the response you need. Even though this can help reduce the risk, there is no way to guarantee a positive response from an Intelligent Vulnerability partner. We can only use our best judgment by considering the questions laid out in this chapter.

A good rule of thumb concerning friendships is to share with them on the level that they are willing to share with you. This does not mean that the person must be open to the same topic but to the same depth. This also doesn't mean they have to be actively working through a vulnerability also. In fact, that would make things significantly more difficult. They just need to be open enough that you are confident you will be safe sharing with them. The healthiest relationships have a history of balanced sharing, and both individuals invest their time and energy toward maintaining this friendship. They can keep the lines of communication open and share genuinely with each other. They both understand they must be willing to make an investment in confidentiality because the information being shared has the potential to cause great pain if this trust is broken.

It's important to note that there are other relationships that don't fit the rule of thumb above. Some examples would be a mentor, parent, relative, or pastor. We must follow the Intelligent Vulnerability process, but they may just be a good partner for us without needing to share equally with us. They may be a trustworthy person who has already found healing for many of their vulnerabilities and have the time to help us work through ours. Sometimes these are good Intelligent Vulnerability partners, but we must remember, sharing with a person in a role of authority doesn't guarantee safety.

The most important piece of information to keep in mind, when asking how much we share, is that we must have appropriate and realistic expectations. The reality is that nobody is perfect. We all have flaws and faults that will inevitably come out at times. We need to be prepared for it because no matter how hard we try or how closely we try to follow the guidelines laid down in this book, there will come a time when someone unintentionally responds in a way that may hurt the person who is sharing. The key is two-fold: understanding that this is bound to occur, and you having established trust and strength in the relationship, so that it can withstand this slip-up. This is when we must apologize and ask for forgiveness.

As important as these suggestions are to help us answer the question about what and how much to share, they remain suggestions. We all know that there is no way to guarantee our success or safety when delving into issues of the heart and sharing them with other people. I can tell you from personal experience that if you apply these faithfully in your life and relationships, you will significantly reduce the risk of being hurt further and enhance the chances that you will begin finding healing to your heart's deepest vulnerabilities.

Possible need for professional help

All of this sounds pretty good on paper, but we need to take great care to understand how this works in the real world. The hard truth is that some of us don't have the kind of relationships that can handle this kind of vulnerability. Others of us have pain and struggles that are so deep that it would be unfair of us to ask those around us to help carry our burden. These would be the kind of issues that would be best dealt with by a professional.

There is no shame in looking to a counselor or therapist when needing help working through many of these vulnerabilities. In fact, well-trained counselors will provide an environment of safety that can rarely be matched anywhere outside of the therapy room. They have a formal education in helping people work through their issues with the least amount of risk. There are even laws and professional ethics that attempt to make sure confidentiality is kept and no harm is done. If you need these assurances when it comes to certain vulnerabilities, then spending the money for these professional services would best fit your situation. Just remember that just like in every other field, not all counselors excel at their job. It might take some time to find a good therapist that is the right fit for you.

If I had gone in for professional counseling, it is likely that the process of coming to grips with my disability may have occurred at a faster pace, but I also may have lost out on some of the amazing conversations that ultimately played a part in my healing and led to deeper, more intimate relationships with those whom I shared my vulnerability with.

You can gain great confidence by exercising your newfound knowledge concerning whether you are ready to open the gate of your heart to others. Remember, you must be in control of your gate because it is what allows those closest to you to be given access to your vulnerabilities. Our gates are the primary way we manage the risk of deciding whom to share our hearts with. In the next chapter, we will expand on the concept of the gate to our hearts. We will do this by looking at who to trust and what character qualities they should possess.

Key Concepts

First Big Question: Are my motives for sharing my vulnerabilities with those I care about most, positive or negative?

Emotional vulnerability with others is not always good. It can be either a positive or a negative experience.

Second Big Question: Do I need to be Intelligently Vulnerable?

Three True or False statements.
1. My vulnerability is negatively affecting my life or my relationships with others.
2. I spend considerable time maintaining my image.
3. I realize that I need to confront my vulnerability to move forward in my life and find freedom to be my best self.

If you answered true to at least parts of these, then there are three more questions.
1. Are you willing to make the time required to ponder and talk through your vulnerabilities?
2. Are you ready to put out the effort it takes to work through a specific vulnerability or vulnerabilities?
3. Are you confident the potential reward outweighs the potential risks involved?

The reality is that Intelligent Vulnerability takes work, and working through hard and painful issues takes discipline and commitment. There's no shame in answering that you are not ready to confront your vulnerabilities at this time.

Third Big Question: Are you ready to take responsibility for what and how much you share?

Remember, there is no way to guarantee your success or safety when delving into issues of the heart and sharing them with other people. You must assume that responsibility.

Discussion Points (Group)

What are some positive motives for emotional vulnerability?

What are some negative motives for emotional vulnerability?

What relationships should we consider for an Intelligent Vulnerability partner?

What are some factors to consider when deciding when to start sharing your heart?

What are some ways we can manage the risk concerning what and how much we share?

Getting Personal (Just for you)

Do you want to be emotionally vulnerable with others for the right reasons?

Have you ever chosen to be emotionally vulnerable for the wrong reasons? To the wrong person?

What relationships in your life might make good Intelligent Vulnerability partners?

Do you have a vulnerability you might be ready to share with your most trusted person? If so, are you prepared to manage the risk?

9
How Do You Know Who to Trust?

Where do we look?

The most obvious place to find someone we trust is our circle of friends. One of the primary reasons we consider them friends is because we trust them. We can count on them to be there when we need them. However, just because someone is your friend or spouse does not guarantee that person will make a good Intelligent Vulnerability partner. Just think about your circle of friends for a minute. You probably have a friend who would come to help you paint your house, but you would not ask them to watch your kids. You may have another friend who would love to help you redecorate your home but wouldn't want to help build a new deck; we all have different gifts and talents. While everybody might benefit from being Intelligently Vulnerable, this might not be the right time for them, and not everyone is equally prepared to engage in it.

We need to look for our friends who place great value on not just what's going on in our lives, but what's going on in our hearts. This person needs to be willing to engage with us on a deeper level. We need to understand and accept that friends like this are hard to come by in today's fast-paced and superficial culture. We also need to understand that just because your friend is not willing or equipped does not make them a bad friend. In the same way, if your spouse is the one who is unwilling or unequipped to engage you, this does not mean that you have a bad marriage. Marriages, like friendships, can look very different but be equally meaningful. Many men, and some women, struggle to talk openly and share their hearts, but may still love intensely. It is important to note here that being able to be Intelligently Vulnerable with our spouse is not the only way to find intimacy and oneness in your marriage. Marriages, just like friendships, can be happy and healthy in a variety of different ways. Whether we are sharing with our spouse or a close friend, the reality is, we often need help standing up to the truth about ourselves. We need someone who can both listen to our hearts and reflect the truth back to us in a safe way.

Before we move forward and look specifically at the trust needed for Intelligent Vulnerability, we need to address what may be the biggest trap concerning emotional vulnerability. It is the false idea that a romantic relationship is the ideal place to engage in Intelligent Vulnerability. This could not be further from the truth because romance and Intelligent Vulnerability are troublesome partners. They are not necessarily compatible, especially during early dating. This is a time when emotions are flying high, and hormones are raging. We are often blinded by our emotions from seeing any yellow, or even red flags. Of course, we can't be in a romantic relationship without opening our hearts but try to keep it to the emotionally transparent level.

We can share a whole lot about who we are by being transparent and genuine. Save any true emotional vulnerability until there has been a significant level of trust and commitment built.

Let's take this one step further. Just because someone is in love with us does not mean that they are a person who is or can be an Intelligent Vulnerability partner. Marriage does not guarantee that our husband or wife will be a safe or enthusiastic partner in the Intelligent Vulnerability process. While marriage would seem to be the ideal place for Intelligent Vulnerability to be practiced, it is not the only place, nor is it always the best in every situation. There is still a very important role for close friends, preferably more than one, to help us work through our deepest vulnerabilities. You will find that initially, there may only be one person who you feel safe enough to share with at the deepest level, but as you begin healing you might have conversations with other friends on a specific aspect of your vulnerability. Remember when I shared about asking Ken how my disability affected our friendship after he became my part-time caregiver? This is a perfect example because while we were good friends, I didn't regularly talk to him about my vulnerability. But I did trust him to answer my question in an honest and caring way. It's important to note that the Intelligent Vulnerability process is fluid and there isn't one right way to work through it. We are only setting guidelines to help make it as safe as possible. So, the way I have gone through the process will look a little different from the way you go through it. In fact, there is no research or proof that Intelligent Vulnerability, as I have defined it, works at all. Only that it worked for me, and I believe it can work for you too.

If you are married or are in a committed relationship, and your Intelligent Vulnerability partner is NOT your spouse or significant other, then Intelligent Vulnerability is typically best practiced in same-gender friendships, particularly in the early stages when the emotions are the deepest. You must be aware that intimate sharing with the opposite gender can be dangerous because it can lead to physical intimacy. We must also be careful to avoid an emotional affair. This occurs when spouses share deeply intimate feelings about themselves and their marriage with someone of the opposite gender who is not their spouse. It is very important that we avoid breaking that marital trust either physically or emotionally.

If you are single, I still believe Intelligent Vulnerability is best practiced in same-gender friendships. The most important reason for this is stability. It's much easier to be committed to a same-gender friend. You don't have to worry about becoming romantic and potentially breaking up, or that one of you becomes romantically involved with someone else and that person isn't comfortable with the level of intimacy you two share. Typically, same-gender friendships last through the breakups and are still there after you get married. This person would have the quality we will discuss shortly, which is commitment.

"One another" commands

As we begin looking at the qualities most important in the Intelligently Vulnerable relationship we will start with the Bible. It is full of "one another" commands and is the ultimate source of truth. I can't think of anywhere better to find some great examples of what it means to live life together or for the purpose of this book to be Intelligently Vulnerable. Sadly, in today's culture, it's nearly impossible to live some of these out in the world and even sometimes in a church body. But we can live them out in one-on-one relationships and then carry what we've learned into the world, especially into the church. You see, once we have found healing for our vulnerability, then we are no longer vulnerable to the emotions that went with it, but it has been transformed into a diamond. It becomes transparent and we can share our story with others, as I have done here. The verses that follow are not an exhaustive list of "one another" commands but merely the ones I believe are important qualities for the Intelligently Vulnerable relationship.

Kindness, compassionate, forgiving – Ephesians 4:32; Colossians 3:13

Humility - 1 Peter 5:5; Philippians 2:3

Don't judge - Romans 14:13

Acceptance - Romans 15:7

Encourage - 1 Thessalonians 4:18; 5:11; Hebrews 3:13; 10:25

Builds you up - 1 Thessalonians 5:11

Servant's heart - Galatians 5:13

There is one more command that is probably the most famous of them all and it plays a huge role in being a safe person in the Intelligent Vulnerability process. We call it the Golden Rule and it was from the lips of Jesus. Matthew 7:12 says, *"So in everything, do to others what you would have them do to you, for this sums up the Law and the Prophets."* It's obvious how this applies to an Intelligent Vulnerability relationship, but also, once we have given and received this kind of grace, then we are more able to pass on that grace to a co-worker who may be treating you badly because they are having a difficult time in their own life. Or maybe it's a parent on your child's sports team who just isn't a very good person. You are better able to overlook their pettiness and not take it personally. The Intelligent Vulnerability process is not only about healing and more intimate relationships, but it also better prepares us to live out these "one another" commands in our everyday lives, both with those we choose to spend time with and those chosen for us.

I encourage you to take a personal inventory and ask yourself how many of these qualities you possess. If you find yourself lacking, then you must ask the Lord to help you grow in those areas. It's not only important that your Intelligent Vulnerability partner possess these qualities, but you must also possess them yourself. How can we expect others to be safe if we aren't working to be safe ourselves? This brings us to the key issue concerning Intelligent Vulnerability, which is trust. We will find the Biblical qualities we just looked at all throughout this next section.

Key Issues:
Trust

How can I identify which friends I can trust in the Intelligent Vulnerability process? In staying with our analogy of a gate to our hearts, I would say TRUST should be the lock on our gates. You should never even consider unlocking your gate until a significant amount of trust has been built. In our world today we have locks that require a code to unlock. There are four primary qualities that should act as the code to your gate. You must assess whether your potential Intelligent Vulnerability partner possesses these four qualities that will help you assess how trustworthy they are. These are certainly not the only qualities, but they are the ones I believe are the most important.

Respect

The first quality is respect. *Will this person respect the access they are given to come behind my wall?* The gate into your heart and behind your emotional wall should always be under your control. In the Intelligent Vulnerability process, you are either the person inside who controls the gate or the person outside of the gate waiting to be invited inside. Being invited inside should be considered an honor, and we must respect the entry we are given.

Discuss expectations and set some ground rules. Here is a common basic plan. Be willing to listen at length to each other, but don't make comments or give advice without receiving permission. We should ask for permission if we intend to say or bring something to the attention of the one owning the vulnerability, particularly early in the Intelligent Vulnerability relationship. This could include saying, "Can I share with you something I'm noticing?" or "When you're ready to hear them, I have some thoughts I would like to share with you."

Another point is this: A good Intelligent Vulnerability partner does not try to persuade us to their point of view. They understand the importance of giving options instead of advice. When I was a Christian Counselor and now as a dad or a friend, I encourage people to avoid giving advice because this places the responsibility of the outcome on the advice giver. It is much better to give options, instead, because this allows the person to make their own choice and to be responsible for that choice. They are also more likely to follow through on the matter if they feel like they have chosen the answer for themselves.

Lastly, our primary role as an Intelligent Vulnerability partner is as a listener and not a fixer or a problem-solver. Access allows us to listen, but permission allows us to speak and provide options, not solutions. Arguments may be made once the Intelligent Vulnerability relationship is well established, but being too eager to build the case for your viewpoint may be an indicator that you have failed to understand the process.

Integrity

The second quality is integrity. *Does this person have integrity?* You need to ask the question: Is he or she truthful? Does this person tend to embellish (stretch) the truth? There is no need to add extra risk by sharing our vulnerability with someone who does not understand the importance of honesty.

Has the person shown him or herself to be responsible? Does the individual take responsibility for his or her life and actions, or is this person prone to blame others? Friends who make good Intelligent Vulnerability partners are strong enough to take responsibility for both positive and negative interactions.

Do they tend to gossip? Do they tend to repeat things that others have told them in confidence? There is no room in the Intelligent Vulnerability relationship for someone who is likely to break our confidence and share our vulnerabilities with others.

Do they tend to wear a mask? Do they act one way around you, another way at work, and yet another way at church? These people are like a chameleon and make themselves fit into whatever situation they are in. This person has a desire to fit in and be liked, making this person a bad candidate for an Intelligent Vulnerability Partner.

Do they have a positive or negative impact on those in their company? When confiding your innermost vulnerabilities to someone, it's essential that they have a positive influence on you and that their friendship encourages and motivates you.

Commitment

The third quality is commitment. *Are they willing to make a commitment and follow through with it?* When you open up and share your vulnerabilities with someone, it's crucial that they're willing to stick by your side, even when things get tough. Healing and personal growth can be challenging, but having a committed partner who is dedicated to being a part of your journey is important.

Will this person take your vulnerabilities seriously and consistently over time? It is important that you understand this process usually doesn't occur over days or weeks, but rather months and sometimes years. You need someone who is committed to being a consistent part of your life. However, we understand that people cannot make promises about the future because the future is in God's hands, not ours. But we can state our good intentions, as long as we are able to help.

Does this person have the time to commit? The primary person you engage with in the Intelligent Vulnerability process needs to be able to spend at least an hour of their time listening and talking on a regular basis. It might be a good idea to discuss the amount of time your partner and you have available before starting each discussion and set a time limit. Otherwise, things could go much longer than your partner expects, thereby discouraging them from wanting to meet again. Or your partner might interrupt saying that they've got to go, leaving you feeling embarrassed, thus being awkward for both of you.

If you find a partner who qualifies in the other areas but does not have time for you currently, then consider sharing with this person in the future, when they are available.

Is this person committed to helping you find your own answers? Do they tend to correct or advise quickly, wanting to solve the issue and move on? This question hits close to home for me more than any other. As a counselor by trade, and as a man, I have gotten a double dose of the "fix it" trait. I have learned that I have a huge tendency to try to get to the root of the issue and solve it quickly, rather than just listen and come alongside. I have learned the hard way that even though I do this from a desire to help, it can cause the person sharing to close their gate and not want to share anymore. I find myself outside the wall again and must ask for forgiveness. We must be committed to listening and coming alongside first and foremost.

Empathy

The fourth quality is empathy. *Is this person capable of being empathetic?* Empathy is a foundational quality for a good Intelligent Vulnerability partner. We need to be clear that empathy is different from sympathy, and each has a different impact on the Intelligent Vulnerability relationship. Sympathy is something that we do when we're dealing in the realm of transparency. It simply says I agree with you and I'm sorry for what you are going through. Empathy, on the other hand, is something we do when we're dealing in the realm of vulnerability. It means understanding and entering another's feelings, being willing to put yourself in your friend's shoes so that you can attempt to see things from his or her perspective.

Is this person able to listen without passing judgment? Or does this person have biases regarding ethnicity, social status, disability, etc.? We need to have enough common sense to know that if a person tends to judge others, they will probably judge us too.

Is this person willing to admit their own weaknesses? Every one of us has weaknesses and vulnerabilities whether we want to admit them or not. It is unlikely that someone would be able to humbly engage you and show empathy if they think they are perfect.

There may be other traits that come to your mind that have to do with being trustworthy and you can add them to the list. As I mentioned before, this list is not meant to be exhaustive but covers major areas of concern that should be taken into consideration when looking for an Intelligent Vulnerability partner.

In keeping with our analogy of needing a functioning gate within the wall around our hearts, I would say that the key elements of trust are: respect, integrity, commitment, and empathy and are the primary keys you should expect if you are going to unlock your gate and let someone inside your heart and see your vulnerabilities. And remember, you also must ask yourself if these qualities are present in you.

Seriously, do you possess these qualities? If not, then you need to begin working now to make them yours. Most of us are likely to have at least one area that we struggle with, and it is vital that you recognize this and begin consciously working on improving it. I am still working on overcoming my "fix it" mentality even as I write this, and I'm old enough to know that I will continue to find areas that I need to grow in to become a better Intelligent Vulnerability partner. We should always be working on overcoming weaknesses and faults as we become aware of them.

You have now completed the last step in the Intelligent Vulnerability process. It is now up to you to decide what you're going to do with it.

In the next chapter, I will teach you some counseling techniques that are very useful in the Intelligent Vulnerability relationship—Attending Behavior and Reflective Listening. Also, we will briefly talk about the role of Intelligent Vulnerability in small groups.

Key Concepts

Being a spouse or good friend does not guarantee that person will make a good Intelligent Vulnerability partner.

Romantic relationships are NOT the best place for Intelligent Vulnerability relationships. It's best to function at the level of emotional transparency until there has been a significant level of trust and commitment built.

If you are married or are in a committed relationship, and your Intelligent Vulnerability partner is NOT your spouse or significant other, then Intelligent Vulnerability is typically best practiced in same-gender friendships, particularly in the early stages when the emotions are the deepest.

If you are single, I still believe Intelligent Vulnerability is best practiced in same-gender friendships. The most important reason for this is stability.

As you begin healing, you might have conversations with other friends on a specific aspect of your vulnerability.

The "one another" commands show us some great qualities for Intelligent Vulnerability relationships.

Trust should act as the lock for your gate. The four qualities that should be the code for our lock are Respect, Integrity, Commitment, and Empathy. Use RICE to help you remember them.

Remember, you're not only looking for these qualities in an Intelligent Vulnerability partner, but you should possess them yourself.

Discussion Points (Group)

Where should we look to find a good Intelligent Vulnerability partner?

Are romantic relationships a good place to practice Intelligent Vulnerability? Marriage? Explain

Apart from marriage, do you agree or disagree that Intelligent Vulnerability is best practiced in same-gender friendships. Explain

What kind of qualities do the "one another" commands require of us?

How do we protect our hearts from others?

How do we know who might be safe enough to enter our gates?

What's the code to the lock?

Getting Personal (Just for you)

Who might be a good Intelligent Vulnerability partner for you?

Do they possess the "one another" characteristics? Do you possess them?

Which "one another" characteristic do you need to become better at?

Do you know someone who is trustworthy? Are you trustworthy?

Do you know someone who has RICE characteristics? Do you have RICE characteristics?

Section 3

Tips, Purposes, and Proofs Intelligent Vulnerability Works

10
Some Important Tips

In this chapter, we'll learn some basic listening skills. These skills will help you be a better Intelligent Vulnerability partner. Also, some form of a small group ministry has become an important part of many churches today, therefore, we will look at the role they play in our growth.

Listening skills

First, we must *listen with our body through attending behavior.* Attending behavior is a physical orientation toward Intelligent Vulnerability partners. These behaviors reinforce the notion that we are paying attention and listening to them and are genuinely interested in what they are sharing.

These behaviors include the following:

1. Eye Contact—Maintain eye contact, but don't lock into a stare. Eye contact is a part of our facial expression. We normally follow an interesting conversation with our expressions, such as smiling or wrinkling or raising the brow. This is probably the most important behavior that communicates our genuine interest in what they are sharing.

A grandfather was reading the newspaper as his young granddaughter was telling him something. She kept talking, he kept reading. "Are you listening to me?" she would ask every few sentences. He would say, "I'm listening." Finally, after repeated attempts to get a stronger commitment from him, she said, "But papa, I want you to listen to me with your eyes."

2. Proximity—This is how close we are to the other person. We should stay at a conversational distance, which constitutes not being in the person's face, but also not across the room.

3. Posture—It is best to stay in a position that allows us to maintain eye contact. We should maintain an open posture (no folded arms across the chest). We also need to sit comfortably but without slouching. Leaning forward toward the person is good but avoid sitting with your head down.

4. Gestures—We communicate a great deal with body movements. Relax and use gestures that are appropriate for the conversation. Head nods and hand gestures are OK, but avoid nervous habits, such as drumming fingers, picking nails, or checking text messages, as they can be distracting.

Second, we must *listen with verbal cues*. Confirm that you are listening with sounds and short acknowledgments as you listen. These are the verbal punctuation of conversation and include words or expressions such as: really, um, hmm, oh yeah, groans (in sympathy) and short laughs. It is also natural to make short statements that show you are engaged with them such as: "That must be difficult" or "I'm sorry you had to go through that." Remember to be natural in using these cues because using them too often will be distracting and possibly annoying.

Third, in good listening, we *allow for times of silence*. We need to give our Intelligent Vulnerability partner a chance to pause, and then continue. This can be difficult, but it is an important way you can support your Intelligent Vulnerability partner. This communicates that your focus remains on listening to them and what they have to say. We are often uncomfortable with silence, so if the sharer pauses for even a short time, we sometimes feel the need to say something. Sometimes people just need a moment or even a minute to gather their thoughts. Typically, if the sharer is done talking, they will ask for your feedback. Another important note is this: not all situations require you to respond verbally, particularly in times of crisis. My dad used to say, "sometimes the most powerful thing you can do for a person who is struggling is just to sit with them." He called it the "ministry of presence." We must get comfortable with silence.

Attending behavior not only communicates our interest but also helps us to genuinely listen. Orientating our body helps us to fully engage our minds and emotions. While these behaviors are valuable, they should not be seen as requirements. Use them as helpful tips as you develop your style in order to be natural.

Caring attitude

We not only need to maintain a physical orientation toward an Intelligent Vulnerability partner, but we also need to orientate our attitude as well.

First, we must *exhibit an attitude of empathy and acceptance.*

1. Listen with empathy. We are trying to understand the Intelligent Vulnerability partner's thoughts and feelings from his or her point of view.

2. Listen with acceptance. This is listening to your partner without judgment. This is especially important when a vulnerability is first being shared. We need to reaffirm our acceptance and non-judgment to help our Intelligent Vulnerability partner through difficult moments.

3. Listen without pretense. Be open about who and what you are as it is appropriate. The more we are genuinely ourselves, the more freedom our partner feels to be him or herself. If our partner's spin-self is talking to our spin-self, then we aren't going to make any progress.

Second, practice *reflective listening*. This means that we listen and verbally reflect back to the Intelligent Vulnerability partner what we are hearing and understanding. This process, sometimes called restatement or active listening, helps us make sure we have heard what the other person is saying and feeling. It also reassures the sharer that the listener has heard what he or she is saying and feeling. If the sharer has been misunderstood, it also allows them an opportunity to try again to share their thoughts. We practice reflection through repeating, rephrasing, or paraphrasing what we have heard. This process includes not only the facts of what is being said but also the emotions surrounding how the Intelligent Vulnerability partner feels.

This is important because understanding our partner's emotions allows us to empathize with him or her. We understand where our partner is coming from. Do you remember the difference between empathy and sympathy? We have not really heard someone until we have heard their feelings. This means not just hearing their words but feeling their struggle with certain emotions.

This also helps an Intelligent Vulnerability partner to clarify his or her thoughts, because sometimes, having to verbalize thoughts and emotions helps us to realize precisely what we think and feel. If we have listened well, using reflective listening, we will be able to accurately summarize what our partner has said including his or her feelings associated with the vulnerability.

Mirroring

Our last point here is a concept called *mirroring*, which I believe is one of the most powerful tools we can use in the Intelligent Vulnerability process. This term is used in different ways in the counseling and psychotherapy world. Some use it to refer to what we just talked about—reflective listening. Others use the term to refer to the technique whereby we mimic another person's behaviors so he or she feels more comfortable.

However, I want to use it in a different way here. All of us have probably put a mirror in the sunlight and reflected the bright light of the sun onto a wall or onto someone. As Intelligent Vulnerability partners, we are the living mirrors through which God's truth is reflected to another person. We can attempt to see those around us through the eyes of Christ and reflect God's promises and God's truth concerning how profoundly unique and loved that person is.

It is also our responsibility to look for positive traits in others and reflect those back to them. Sometimes amid our struggles, we have difficulty seeing our strengths and can get focused on our perceived weaknesses. We need someone to speak encouragement into our lives and restore a sense of hope. Other times our vulnerabilities keep us from seeing our potential. Helping someone to see their potential might even change the course of their life. This is a privilege and a responsibility.

When we understand the spiritual truth about ourselves and our Christian brothers and sisters, we learn that we are made in the image of God—fearfully and wonderfully made. We are forgiven of sins and have a new identity as children of God. We are co-heirs with Christ our Lord. When we "catch" that truth, much like the way we can catch the light with a mirror, and reflect that truth back to someone, it can have a powerful effect.

When we are burdened with all the things that weigh us down, especially our vulnerabilities, it is easy to forget who we are. But there is no spin in the truth of our identity in Christ, and there is no place for the spin-self. This pure truth cleanses our souls and gives us hope in our worst circumstances. Perhaps reflecting God's truth back to someone is the simplest way to be our brother's keeper. Intelligently Vulnerable relationships provide the context for us to reinforce God's love for someone in a deeply personal way—eye-to-eye and heart-to-heart.

Intelligent Vulnerability and small group community

Intelligent Vulnerability does not replace or reduce the need for Christian small group life. Small groups are necessary for a variety of reasons and provide us with some essential benefits. These small groups are becoming more and more vital because our world is becoming more individualized and isolated. As technology continues to grow, we find ourselves in a cyber world. We have our smartphones, our laptops, our tablets, and some have virtual reality headsets. We work extremely long hours and many worship the almighty dollar. We have lost, to a large degree, most of our sense of community with those around us. We find that we don't truly know anyone.

On a basic level, small groups fill our need for social relationships. They are often a place where we learn how to fit in, to belong, and to tell "our story." When a group is functioning properly, it levels the playing field. Each member has an equal claim to care and protection from the group. Each member also has equal value and ownership in the group. It is here that we learn how to live with, forgive, love, and care for people who are like us, who are different from us, who inspire us, and who try our patience. We can observe how those in the group interact with others on a social and personal level and learn from them. These groups may also give us a great place to meet someone who may have the potential to end up being a great Intelligent Vulnerability partner.

While there is great value in small groups, they cannot safely replace our need for close, personal relationships. Group settings are not the place for dealing with issues that require confidentiality beyond a very basic level. The reality is that the more people you share with, the greater the risk that someone will betray a confidence. Common sense would tell us, if we were in a group of 10 to 12 people, it wouldn't be wise to open our hearts and share our vulnerabilities.

Groups should never be a place where people are encouraged to "tell all," Nor should they be a place where people should be expected to "hear all." One important rule to live by is we should not share something that would threaten our comfort level or future participation in the group if our confidence is betrayed. Our deepest vulnerabilities would be best shared in a safe place with an Intelligent Vulnerability partner. We should primarily function in the realm of transparency in most group settings.

Small groups are an adequate environment for us to learn transparency, but not for being vulnerable. Do you remember our definition of transparency from Chapter 1? Emotional transparency is sharing an aspect of ourselves with minimal risk because there is no invitation for another person to come inside our emotional wall. We open our gate and let others see in a little, but we don't invite them behind our wall. We likened this to opening the door of your home just a little to see who is there—and maybe have a short conversation at the door. But normally, unless we know the person or have another good reason to invite the person inside, we keep the conversation at the door.

Transparency in small groups should be that "at the door" level of sharing. Even at this level, it will still involve some risks—risk is unavoidable when dealing with anything concerning our hearts. When sharing at this level, we should remain relatively safe, although groups do vary in their capacity for transparency, and this is a judgment call. It is important to know your group and weigh the risks. If you are unsure about sharing something, then don't. Instead, consider sharing with someone you feel safe with and follow the Intelligent Vulnerability process. We should also note that if we or someone in the group practices transparency, the other members of the group should take on the collective responsibility to defend that member from other members of the group if they try to take advantage of the transparency to evaluate, insult, attack, criticize, initiate gossip, or any other negative behaviors.

As a rule, Intelligent Vulnerability is not compatible with group settings. The only exception would be a *closed*, well-managed group that offers a considerable measure of safety. These would primarily be groups overseen by trained facilitators or professional counselors. There could also be others though, such as a same-sex accountability group with 3 to 5 members. Remember, if the group has both men and women in it, the risk is greatly increased. The key is that it must be a closed group and a high level of trust must be established between each member, and confidentiality expected. This is quite rare, which is why Intelligent Vulnerability will always be best practiced on a one-on-one basis.

Key Concepts

We should try to use attending behaviors, which is a physical orientation towards our Intelligent Vulnerability partner. These include eye contact, proximity, posture, and gestures.

Listen with verbal cues which are sounds and short acknowledgements.

Listen by allowing for times of silence which allows your Intelligent Vulnerability partner to pause and then continue.

We must also have a caring attitude toward our partner.

Listen with empathy, acceptance, and without pretense.

Reflective listening is listening and verbally reflecting back to the Intelligent Vulnerability partner what we are hearing and understanding.

We used the term mirroring as a way of looking for positive traits in others and reflecting those back to them, especially the truth about who God says we all are if we are believers in Jesus.

Intelligent Vulnerability does not replace or reduce the need for Christian small group life.

Small groups should function at the level of emotional transparency where genuine sharing occurs, but not at the deeper emotional vulnerability level.

As a rule, Intelligent Vulnerability is not compatible with most group settings. The only exception would be a *closed*, well-managed group that offers a considerable measure of safety.

Discussion Points (Group)

What are some attending behaviors? Can you think of any others not listed here?

What are some challenges of allowing for times of silence when listening?

What are some ways we can have a caring attitude towards our Intelligent Vulnerability partner?

What is reflective listening? Have you ever used it? Try practicing it using transparency.

How do we use the term mirroring? Do you think this can positively impact others?

How would it feel if someone told you some positive traits about yourself? Let's try it here in a transparent way.

What are some reasons Intelligent Vulnerability doesn't fit well with small groups? What are some exceptions?

What are some reasons we need small group life? What emotional level should we function at here?

Getting Personal (Just for you)

Are you willing to practice attending behaviors in your Intelligent Vulnerability conversations?

Are you willing to work on allowing for times of silence when listening?

What kind of attitude do you have towards others? Do you need to have a more caring attitude?

Are you willing to practice reflective listening?

Are you willing to look for positive traits in others and be an encourager to them through mirroring?

11
Freedom, Oneness, and Faith

Throughout this book, we have focused primarily on two results that come from Intelligent Vulnerability and they build upon one another. First, we work on developing deeper, more intimate relationships where we are truly known and truly know those closest to us. Second, amid these Intelligently Vulnerable relationships, we find healing for some of our deepest vulnerabilities. But there is a third result that may be the most profound of all. It is that as we find healing from our vulnerabilities, we find the freedom to be our true selves.

Healing brings freedom

The weeks and months that followed the start of my Intelligent Vulnerability process were much the same as those before them, except for one little thing: I was gradually becoming more and more comfortable in my own skin. I was beginning to see myself in a more honest way. I was beginning to stop listening to my spin-self and starting to listen to the voice of the Lord. For the first time in my life, I was beginning to have the courage to look at myself and see the real Chris, the Chris with disabilities.

In the past, I needed to see myself as a normal person, no different from the next person. I was never treated like a person with disabilities, nor did I want to be. Of course, I knew that I was a person with physical limitations, but I fought with everything in me to see myself as just a regular guy. I rarely asked for special privileges and often did things the hard way just to be able to do them with my friends.

It was during this time that I realized how deep this need was to be accepted as one of the guys. I constantly needed to prove to myself that I was normal, and this fact was seen very clearly by the type of girls that I dated in college. I always went for the beautiful girls in school. Many of my fraternity brothers used to give me a hard time because they would say that I always had a better-looking date than they did. I must admit that I did go out on dates with some wonderful women who were beautiful inside and out. If any of those ladies are reading this, know that I thought you had some great qualities. But I felt I needed to prove something to those around me. "Hey, I may be in a wheelchair, but I'm worthy enough to date beautiful women too."

It was not until about this time that I realized that my need to take out only beautiful women really had nothing to do with my need to prove something to others. But it had everything to do with my need to prove to myself that I was normal, that I was a man. I came to realize that I didn't need to prove anything to my family and my friends; I just needed to begin to see myself and accept myself the way they saw me and accepted me. This is what I mean when I say I'm now able to see myself as the disabled Chris. It means that my disability is as much a part of who I am as the color of my hair or lack thereof. No longer was I a disabled person trying to be normal, but I could now say I'm a normal person who just happened to be disabled. Whew! What a relief! I no longer had to hide, and I no longer had to pretend to be something I was not. Although I had been a Christian for well over a decade, I had still been trying to define myself when it came to the vulnerability of my disability. Even though I had been working to find my identity in Christ, I learned that there was no freedom in any area I didn't surrender to Him. It was only after I admitted my vulnerabilities and found healing through Intelligent Vulnerability that I found freedom. I had finally found the freedom to begin truly being who God had created me to be.

There is something deep inside us that puts tremendous value on freedom. We will fight to the end to protect it. In fact, many people don't want to accept Jesus because they don't want to give up what they perceive as freedom. I always think of that final scene in *Braveheart* where William Wallace cries out one last time, "F-R-E-E-D-O-M!" The crowd roars with approval. As motivational as this scene may be, true freedom is not found here. This freedom is still defined by the self. True freedom is only found when we can once again allow the Lord to define who we are.

In the same way, though we may learn to cope, we can only find real freedom in the message of the Gospel. The Gospel of Jesus Christ, the good news about Him, begins our journey away from self.

Using the Bible as our guide, we know the ultimate problem is sin. The core of the gospel is the atoning sacrifice of Christ, which frees us from Satan's power over us, frees us from the penalty of sin, and frees us from the grip of death. When we submit to God, confess our sins, and accept Jesus as our personal Savior, then we are given new life. He begins healing us from our human brokenness. We are given a new identity as we enter an adoptive relationship with God, as His sons and daughters. He restores not only our relationship with Himself, but God makes it possible to have authentic relationships with others—without the masks, without having to pretend to be other than we are. We are free to be ourselves if we will only believe who He tells us we are. We are called to begin letting those closest to us behind our walls—even if it starts with only opening our gates a bit wider.

So, who does God say we are if Jesus is our Lord and Savior? Let's look at a list of Bible verses to find the answer.

You were created in the image of God - Genesis 1:27

He knows everything about you – Psalms 139:1

He knows the number of hairs on your head – Matthew 10:29-31

He knew you before you were conceived – Jeremiah 1:4

He knit you together in your mother's womb – Psalms 139:13

You were not a mistake, for all your days are written in His book – Psalms 139:15-16

You are called a child of God – 1 John 3:1

He loves you with an everlasting love – Jeremiah 31:3

He rejoices over you with singing – Zephaniah 3:17

You are His treasured possession – Exodus 19:5

He loves you so much he sent His son to die for you – John 3:16

No matter where you are in your walk with the Lord or on the journey to Intelligently Vulnerable relationships, it will serve you well to define your identity based on who God says you are. If you find your value in the Lord, then you don't have to depend on anything in this world to give you value. Therefore, there is no amount of success and no amount of failure that can change who you are or how much you're worth.

But God doesn't say that since all these things are true there is nothing else for us to do. He doesn't leave us to continue living the same way we have always lived. Rather, He commands us to respond to His great love by a changed life, growing more like Him daily. We are called to die to our old selves and the sin and self-centeredness that have kept us in bondage.

Let's look at Ephesians 4:22-25 and Colossians 3:9-10 for some more insight.

Eph 4:22 "You were taught, with regard to your former way of life, to put off your old self, which is being corrupted by its deceitful desires; 23 to be made new in the attitude of your minds; 24 and to put on the new self, created to be like God in true righteousness and holiness. 25 Therefore each of you must put off falsehood and speak truthfully to your neighbor, for we are all members of one body."

Col 3:9 "Do not lie to each other, since you have taken off your old self with its practices 10 and have put on the new self, which is being renewed in knowledge in the image of its Creator."

We must begin listening to the voice of Jesus instead of the voice of the spin-self, which is part of the old self, when defining who we are. As we submit ourselves to God, the grip of the old self begins to lose its grip on us. In fact, we are no longer bound to this old way of thinking. We can overcome it. We are called to confront this old self that was born in the garden and put it to death, but it doesn't die easily, and it doesn't go down without a fight. The struggle remains, but it will change as we accept the challenge to be changed. 2 Corinthians 5:17 tells us, *"Therefore, if anyone is in Christ, the new creation has come: The old has gone, the new is here!"* But we must still learn to trust what Christ tells us is the truth concerning who we are and how much we are worth.

Unfortunately, we won't be completely new until we are glorified when we get to heaven. In the meantime, we must allow Jesus to transform us. Romans 12:2 says, *"Do not conform to the pattern of this world, but be transformed by the renewing of your mind. Then you will be able to test and approve what God's will is—his good, pleasing and perfect will."*

Of course, personal Bible study, prayer, and worship are the most essential pieces of Christian growth, but there are, no doubt, godly relationships that are also part of the equation. An Intelligent Vulnerability partner can help us in this process by mirroring back to us who we really are and helping us see ourselves the way God sees us.

The voice of the spin-self has less power when we confront it with the truth about ourselves. The truth is that we have been made new and are no longer slaves to sin and our past. We are to use God's standard as we reflect on our identity and worth. As we just saw from Scripture, we are sons and daughters of the Most High God. Heirs to the Kingdom of Heaven. We are fearfully and wonderfully made. God loves us so much that He sent His son to die on the cross so that we could be reconciled to

Him. He knows everything about us, even the number of hairs on our heads, and he loves us and accepts us despite our flaws because Jesus paid the price for all our sins on the Cross of Calvary.

We were not created to live life behind huge walls with broken gates that isolate us from the intimate relationships we were created for. As part of our Christian calling, we are called to live free, authentic lives in community; being transformed into His likeness. Putting others first, not only in service to them but also in being genuine in how we present ourselves. Our genuineness reflects Christ to others.

Can you see how the concept of Intelligent Vulnerability also helps us find freedom in Christ Jesus? I have found this process to be a key element not only in finding freedom but also in becoming more spiritually mature, as I am shaped to be more like Christ.

Intelligent Vulnerability pulls us away from our self-centeredness.

Intelligent Vulnerability weakens the voice of the spin-self.

Intelligent Vulnerability is one of the best ways to confront our spin-self.

Intelligent Vulnerability keeps us from being alone in our struggle against sin.

Intelligent Vulnerability helps us to mature emotionally.

Intelligent Vulnerability provides the context for the same-gender, deep friendships that we all need.

Intelligent Vulnerability provides the context for marriages to potentially experience a deeper sense of oneness.

Intelligent Vulnerability provides the opportunity to find healing for our deepest vulnerabilities.

Intelligent Vulnerability helps us to find the freedom to be ourselves.

We, as Christians, should not be living under what I call a "bushel-basket" mentality. A bushel basket is woven material, so it is not solid. God's word tells us not to hide our light under a bushel basket. If we were to light a candle in a dark room, it would illuminate all that was around it. If we were to place a bushel basket over this candle, we would drastically limit how much of the room would be illuminated. If you are living your life safely in your comfort zone, hiding under a bushel basket, then you have limited your ability to love and accept those closest to you.

However, if you have the courage to venture into Intelligent Vulnerability, then you will slowly begin to raise that bushel basket off your light, and your ability to love and accept yourself and those around you will significantly increase. Your light will begin to shine brighter, and people will be drawn to you. Not because of you, but rather because of Christ shining more brightly through you.

Oneness is a testimony

There is a unique connection between the Christian concept of the Trinity and the way God has created human beings to relate. In the Trinity, we find that the Father, Son, and Holy Spirit are so intimately and uniquely connected that Scripture tells us they are one. In the gospel of John, we find Jesus speaking to this fact as he prays for future believers in John 17:20-23.

John 17:20 "My prayer is not for them alone. I pray also for those who will believe in me through their message, 21 that all of them may be one, Father, just as you are in me, and I am in you. May they also be in us so that the world may believe that you have sent me. 22 I have given them the glory that you gave me, that they may be one as we are one— 23 I in them and you in me—so that they may be brought to complete unity. Then the world will know that you sent me and have loved them even as you have loved me."

In essence, he prays that all believers should live in intimate connection with one another. This oneness should be a testimony to the world about the unique and profound truth found in the Christian faith. This intimate connection with one another is one of the deepest needs of every person. I believe God envisioned the Christian community, more commonly called the church, to be an example of what intimate connection with one another should look like. Do you think that maybe this is what God meant when he called believers to be salt and light in this world?

Do you ever wonder what it would be like if the church stepped-up and began to develop truly intimate connections in which we cared for one another's needs and the needs of others? I'm not talking about churches helping those in need through the church budget, although this is important because Jesus calls us to do that, but rather, I'm wondering if each individual in the church stepped up to love and serve others instead of assuming that's the pastor's job or what the church leaders are supposed to be doing.

I am blessed to be a part of a church that works to serve.

I'll give you a personal example of the body of Christ serving my family.

Due to my physical condition, I am unable to mow our lawn and my wife works full-time as a 1st grade teacher. Our church recognized this need and asked for volunteers to take turns mowing each week for us. This has been such a blessing for us. If we all stepped up like this and served one another and the world around us in this way, I believe the church would become like a bright light that impacts our culture rather than a dim light made dimmer because we are hiding it inside the bushel basket of our church walls.

We do have examples of this kind of connection in our past. I read a book in Seminary called *The Rise of Christianity* and one major premise of the book was that early Christians cared for the sick, the dying, and the outcast. The author speculated that Christianity grew exponentially during two major plagues of the time. These Christians had this kind of faith and this kind of intimate connection with one another. They cared for others, even at the risk of their own lives, when family members had abandoned them and left them to die. Not only were their lives abundantly ministered to, but they were able to reach out and minister to others in a way that profoundly and drastically changed the world they lived in.

The times have changed, the people may have changed, and even the way we live has changed, but the one thing that has remained constant is that people need other people. More specifically, people need others to reach out truthfully, authentically, and genuinely, being willing to accept them exactly where they are. Just as we saw in this story, people must be cared for before they can get well.

I must ask, have we learned the importance of protecting one another's vulnerabilities? Are we ready to see someone crying out for help as an opportunity to be the hands and feet of Jesus? Or are we still tempted to ask people to get well before we care for them?

Jesus loved the unlovable and cared for those in need, and he commands us to do the same. Sadly, many Christians today confuse Jesus' love for unconditional acceptance. Maybe you remember the story of the woman caught in the act of adultery in John 8:3-11. The men of the city had gathered around to stone her to death, as was the custom in the Jewish culture of the time. Jesus challenged them, saying, "He who is without sin cast the first stone." One by one they dropped their stones and walked away.

We read something very important in verses 10-11. *10 "Jesus straightened up and asked her, "Woman, where are they? Has no one condemned you?" 11 "No one, sir," she said. "Then neither do I condemn you," Jesus declared. "Go now and leave your life of sin."*

Jesus told her that he didn't condemn her either, but he went on to tell her to stop living a lifestyle of sin. This is very different than sinning and truly repenting. He is speaking here of knowing something is a sin and choosing to do it anyway. We can't just continue living with unconfessed sin and believe He doesn't care because He loves us. We can't focus so much on God's love that we forget that He is also holy and just and hates sin. We need to bring our sins and our struggles before the Lord, pray for forgiveness, then turn away from our sinful past and live for Jesus.

But we must also remember that the unbeliever does not

know God yet. We can't expect them to change before we're willing to love them and serve them. In fact, it's the opposite. Our loving and serving them should come first with the hope that they might see Christ in us and find their own saving faith in Jesus. I believe Intelligently Vulnerable relationships are one way God provides to help us become the kind of person who loves and serves others.

I don't know where you are in your walk with God but let me encourage you to never stop striving to mature in your faith. Nor do I know where you are in the Intelligent Vulnerability process, but my hope is, you will find healing, more intimate relationships, and freedom to be your best self.

We must use the knowledge that we gain and the relationships we build to strengthen the local church. Christ prays that we are perfect in unity so that unbelievers can see the true God. If our lives together are not glorifying God and leading others to Him, then we have missed the point. We must be impacting the world for Christ.

If you have never accepted Jesus Christ as your own personal Savior, then I pray today is the day. If you are ready to accept Christ as your Savior and Lord just follow what is called the Roman Road to salvation.

Romans 3:23 - *"For all have sinned and fall short of the glory of God."*

Romans 6:23 - *"For the wages of sin is death, but the gift of God is eternal life in Christ Jesus our Lord."*

Romans 5:8 - *"But God demonstrates his own love for us in this: While we were still sinners, Christ died for us."*

Romans 10:13 - *"Everyone who calls on the name of the Lord will be saved."*

Romans 10:9 - *"If you declare with your mouth, "Jesus is Lord," and believe in your heart that God raised him from the dead, you will be saved. "*

If you have done what these verses say, then you just became a Christ follower and heaven is rejoicing! This will change your life more than all the Intelligently Vulnerable relationships in the world! Please don't keep this to yourself. You need to find a Bible-believing church to support you and help you grow in your new faith. Also, start reading your Bible daily. Your journey has just begun, and I couldn't be more excited for you!

We only have one more chapter to go. In the final chapter, I will share with you the rest of my story. You will see how living a lifestyle of Intelligent Vulnerability has continued to help me grow and change as life has brought new challenges my way.

Key Concepts

Intelligently Vulnerable relationships help us find healing from our vulnerabilities which leads to the freedom to be our true selves.

Our ultimate freedom is found in Christ. It will serve you well to define your identity based on who God says you are.

We, as the church, should be a testimony of oneness. We should be loving and serving one another and the world around us.

Discussion Points (Group)

Generally, what kinds of ways do most people struggle with feeling like they are not enough?

What do you value about freedom?

Who does God say you are if you're a Christian?

What are some benefits of Intelligent Vulnerability?

How can we, as the church, love and serve one another and the world around us?

How has Christ changed your life?

Getting Personal (Just for you)

Do you struggle with feeling like you're not enough?

Is there an area in your life where you're trying to prove yourself? Worthy enough? Smart enough? Wealthy enough? Strong enough?

Are you free to be your best self?

If you are a Christian, do you understand who God says you are? Is your identity in Him?

Are you willing to spend some of your free time to love and serve others?

Are you living out your Christian faith in community?

If you don't know Christ as your personal Savior and Lord, would you consider doing this?

12
The Rest of My Story

You might be wondering what my life has looked like in the years that followed the stories I've shared with you. I will give you a clue before I get more specific. I have continued to live a lifestyle of Intelligent Vulnerability. It has become so ingrained in my being that a lot of times I don't even have to think about it. Of course, now and then something bigger than everyday life pops up and I must remind myself to be intentional about the process. But 20 years down the road, I have a good idea of who I can trust and when I need to engage the Intelligent Vulnerability process. The cool thing is now that I've done it many times, most of the structure is still in place. Unfortunately, it doesn't make facing those painful emotions or having those difficult conversations any easier.

Losing my dad

I was 26 and had only been back in Arkansas for about 16 months when tragedy struck my family. My dad had an elders meeting at church that night, so he left work early to check on the dirt road he was having made on our family property. The property was hilly and somehow, he lost control, and he tumbled down the side of the hill and his ATV landed on top of him. My mom found him about 30 minutes later and I can remember her calling me in a panic. I remember her saying "Your dad has been in a serious accident. Pray! Pray! Pray!"

I was concerned but I thought he would be okay. My Uncle Larry came to pick me up and take me to the hospital. But when we got there my brother came up inside my minivan and simply said "he's gone. He didn't make it." I couldn't believe him at first but then my emotions overwhelmed me, and I began wailing from the depths of my soul. I hadn't cried like that ever before nor since. There were already over 20 people standing around the ER entrance. All these people loved my dad and our family. I rolled past everyone and into the ER room where my dad was lying lifeless. I had someone lift my arm to place my hand on him and through my tears I tried to pray. For the first time in my life, I lacked the faith to pray for what I desired. I asked for strength and then asked the Lord to breathe life back into my dad. . . but to no avail.

The good Lord, in his loving providence, chose that September 29, 2003, was the day my dad's time on earth would end. At the time, I didn't understand why God would take him so soon. He was such a great man, one who made the world a better place. I even remember thinking how much I still needed him, especially because of my disability. I can't know all the reasons for God's choice this side of heaven, but you will see shortly one incredible blessing his loss played a part in.

I did all my crying that first night. After that, I reverted to that person who used his faith as a shield. At the visitation and funeral, I was a pillar of strength, looking each person in the eyes and saying all the right things. I even wrote a poem about my dad and read it at the funeral. After about a month I started having periodic low-level nausea. The counselor in me finally saw I hadn't truly been dealing with my grief and it was finding its way out physically. I talked to some of my Intelligent Vulnerability partners, which helped, but I still couldn't bring myself to cry. Well, that was until I watched his video memories. Seeing the old pictures and listening to the songs we chose for the background music finally did the trick. Tears began falling down my cheeks like a waterfall as I grieved my dad. I felt like a huge weight had been lifted off my chest. I found that I needed to watch his video at least every month to help me grieve.

It was finally around a year later that I watched it without crying. It was then I knew I had dealt with my grief. Now don't get me wrong, it's been 20 years now since he went to be with Jesus, and I still miss him with all my heart. And now that I'm older and have kids of my own, sometimes the tears fall easier because I now understand how deeply he loved my brother and me. In fact, I must admit the tears have been falling as I'm writing this story. But today these tears bring a smile to my heart because I know how incredibly blessed I was to have 26 years with the best dad I could have ever asked for.

My dad left an amazing legacy, and I am proud to carry on part of it. I'm going to share one more story that occurred just a few months before he went to heaven. We worked a Christian weekend retreat together and as you can imagine the beds were very hard. I had to wake my dad up 4-5 times a night to help me turn. Now as great a man as he was, he was not a caregiver by nature, and he valued his sleep. For him, taking care of me was a labor of love. So, this was not an ideal situation, however, my dad took care of me that weekend and I don't remember a grumble.

On the drive home, we had a conversation I will never forget. I was sharing some of my hopes and dreams for my life. He just listened until I was done talking and he said the most powerful words I had ever heard. He looked over and said "Son, I can't make all your hopes and dreams come true, but I will do everything in my power to help you achieve them." I've held on to those words all my life and one of the greatest honors of my life was sharing this story with my kids and then telling them the same exact words. Dad, your legacy lives on! I love you!

Love of my life

I joined e-harmony about 2 ½ years later and was matched with a beautiful young lady from California named Lisa. She had attended college at John Brown University in Arkansas and chose to stay here and teach elementary school. We talked on the phone for about two months before we got the opportunity to meet in person. One of the first things we deeply connected on was the experience of losing our dads. Her dad fought cancer most of his adult life. He too loved the Lord with all his heart and left a great legacy of his own. I believe we see a small glimpse of God's providence at work here. The best way to share our dating relationship with you is to share the letter we wrote to each other before meeting in person for the first time.

7-14-2006

And this boy had prayed all his life that God would give to him the most amazing woman he's ever known. He set his standards so high because he only wanted God's best for him. This boy was determined not to settle even if that meant being single all his life. He prayed and prayed, and he looked and looked, but for 29 years she was nowhere to be found. Many, many people heard the cry of this boy's heart and joined him in his prayers. Then it happened... from out of the blue he began talking to this girl. From the very first e-mail he could tell that there was something different about this girl. He couldn't wait for the opportunity to talk to her on the phone, but he didn't want to do anything to scare her away. He knew almost immediately that this was the girl, the only one he wanted to pursue. So only a week into his new three-month membership he closed every other match and asked that no other matches be sent to him. He then asked this girl if he could call her on the telephone. And oh, my goodness. Her voice. The conversation. The comfort. I think I began falling in love with her that very night.

It was like a whirlwind. I could not get enough of her. We talked for hours and hours. My feelings for this girl grew deeper and deeper with each passing conversation. Then one night, or should I say early one morning, May 28, I could not hold my feelings in any longer. I told this girl how much I loved her that night. And that I fully expected to never say those words to another woman. My love continued to grow for this girl day by day, moment by moment. I grew to admire her and respect her in the most profound of ways. Her faith and dependence on God astounded me. Her character is so pure. Her heart is so tender. Her very being inspired me to be the man God is calling me to be.

And now the day has come that they finally get to be together. Yes, both are a little bit anxious, but the excitement is so much greater. This boy can hardly wait to look upon the woman whom God has chosen as his best. To gaze deep into her eyes. To hold her hand. This boy today loves this girl more than he ever thought possible. She is the most beautiful girl in all the land. She is his exquisite beauty. And he delights in her. He longs to love her like no man has ever loved any woman. He yearns to protect her. To support her. To encourage her. To give her everything she's ever wanted. Because this girl is so much more than he ever dreamed or imagined. She is my gift. She is my best friend. And I can't wait to make her my wife.

I love you with all that I am!
Your Prince

7-14-2006

In the beginning, this girl thought she would take a chance and see if she could find love. When she looked and looked it wasn't there. She thought to herself, let's try something else, sit back and see what the Lord does. She was excited to meet new people, but she had no expectations. What she found has taken her breath away. The Lord was good and brought to her this perfect man who was just right for everything the Lord saw she desired in a mate.

What happened along the journey as they began growing changed her heart. She found herself so deeply in love with the Lord for fighting for her and hearing all her desires from the heart. The more she fell in love with the Lord, the deeper her feelings and love grew for this man. Her story is filled with stories of how the two have talked all night (astounding some that there was that much to say), laughed, cried, and have grown so incredibly close in this time. Today, the two shall finally meet each other and see just exactly what the Lord has given to them. Both are nervous. Both have worries. Both love each other. Both know that what they share is real and right. So, this girl will leave in a little bit. Get into her car and come to the man she prayed for her whole life. She will stand face to face with the man who has captivated her heart. She will be in her piece of heaven on earth this weekend.

Your sunshine

The day finally came for us to meet, and she drove down with her best friend, Michelle. The evening was magical, and our connection translated in person flawlessly. We both knew that what we shared was the real deal. So, two weeks later I proposed to her after we enjoyed watching the sunrise under her grandmother's quilted blanket. I also did my best to sing "Love of My Life" by Michael W. Smith. She said, "Yes" to a life together, even though I'm not a good singer at all. We set the date for March 3, 2007. She would continue living in Siloam Springs until January. She then moved to Hot Springs and lived with my mom until we got married. We spent as much time as we could together, as our relationship continued to grow stronger.

The day finally came, March 3, 2007, and it was one of the best days of my life. I was blessed to marry the most amazing woman in the world and one of my biggest prayers had been answered. It was now time to start our life as a married couple and we were both very excited.

Kids

Our journey up to this point was like the storybook romance you watch at the movies. But life is full of both good times and bad, times that are easy and times that are a struggle. We would soon experience both almost simultaneously. While we were engaged, Lisa had a seizure, but we didn't give it much thought until after we were married, and she became pregnant and had more seizures. She was eventually diagnosed with epilepsy, which would add another stressor to our life together. We'll come back to this a little later.

In June we found out Lisa was pregnant, and I was so excited to find out I was going to be a dad. I couldn't wait to tell my family, friends, and just about anyone who would listen. Lisa wasn't sure she could have kids, so it was a total surprise. We had talked about having children and decided that after a year or so we would begin trying, but about three months after we got married Lisa was pregnant. It was amazing but we barely had time to establish ourselves as a married couple. I hoped we could at least make it to our wedding anniversary before the birth.

Caitlan was born on March 12, 2008. It was incredible to see and hold this beautiful baby girl that God had entrusted into our care. She stole my heart from the moment I first laid eyes on her. I was so proud that day but I'm even prouder today. She is now 15 and her love for God and those around her make her beautiful inside and out. I couldn't be any prouder of the amazing and godly young lady she is becoming.

We had decided before we got married that we would try for one child and stop there if that child inherited my FSHD. Well, the good Lord had other plans because about three months after Cait was born, we found out she was pregnant again. This time Lisa told me through tears because she wasn't sure how we were going to handle 2 children that would be 13 months apart.

Ayden was born April 8, 2009. I couldn't believe that God had chosen to bless us with two amazing children. We didn't plan for him, but there's no doubt our life would be incomplete without him. He is 14 now and is more severely affected by FSHD similarly as me. So, he uses a wheelchair to get around. He has never let it get in the way of living his life to the fullest. I could not be any prouder of him for his strength and perseverance. I can't help him like my dad helped me, but I have tried to be a living example that he can follow his dreams and live a fulfilling life also. He too loves the Lord and is growing into an incredible, godly young man.

As you can imagine, those early years were extremely

difficult, especially for Lisa. I really couldn't help her very much until the kids got old enough to listen and obey. We were blessed that the good Lord gave us sweet kids that began sleeping through the night at a very early age. We leaned on my family and her Uncle Keith. He moved to Hot Springs to help us shortly after Ayden was born. He was a huge help, especially because he gave Lisa someone she could count on. Of course, Lisa's mom and sister would fly out to help also but it was impossible for them to help regularly because we chose not to live in California. Keith not only helped with the kids, but he also helped me many times so Lisa didn't have to. Keith may be my uncle-in-law, but I claim him as my own. He is also like a grandpa to my kids as they call him Keke.

Seizures

Lisa's seizures continued to become more frequent and more severe. She saw epilepsy specialists, both in Arkansas and California, and was eventually placed on three very powerful medications. Although the medications helped decrease the frequency of the seizures, she was still having them. Arkansas state law requires someone to be seizure-free for one full year before driving legally again. She had to sign a document at the epilepsy doctor's office that she wouldn't drive. As you can imagine, having her independence taken away was extremely difficult, especially since she was the only driver in our home. This was before Uber and Doordash. Goodness, how much that would have helped during this time.

It was during these years I was grateful that we both loved

God first, even before one another. We had made our marital commitment in this order also. I am certain this commitment is what got us through the hardest times. Those times when life seemed almost impossible or maybe when our emotions told us that we deserved better. We have never talked about divorce, but there have been a few times the thought has gone through both our minds that it might be easier.

Don't get me wrong, we had a lot of good times too during these years. We found a wonderful church and made some great friends in Sunday school. Some of our favorite memories are spending time with this group of people. They also supported us in many ways. We went on fun dates and enjoyed time with our kids. The Lord blessed us through it all. Even those hard times have strengthened our bond, as we found our way through them.

Lisa went to the hospital for a weekend EEG test, where they stopped her medications with the hope of inducing a seizure, so they could see where they were coming from in her brain. In God's providence, they were successful, and the seizures were coming from one specific spot in her brain. This was the best news we could have prayed for, and we did pray a lot. This meant we could consult with a brain surgeon about surgery. One of the world's best brain surgeons was right here in Arkansas and he recommended surgery. We prayed about it and chose the surgery. God used the hands of that brilliant brain surgeon to heal my wife on June 12, 2013. She had to stay on her medications, but her epilepsy doctor began taking away one medication after another until she remained seizure free without any medication. I am grateful the good Lord healed her, because she might not still be here as bad as some of her seizures were.

Move to Northwest Arkansas

About a month after Lisa's surgery, we sat down to have a serious talk and she told me she couldn't see our marriage surviving if we stayed in Hot Springs. There were just too many difficult and painful memories there and she thought we needed a fresh start. Her heart was still in NW Arkansas where the support system she had built throughout college and as a teacher was. It was difficult for me to leave living in the same town as my family, but I knew she had already sacrificed her support system for me, so it was my turn. I loved her and would have been willing to do whatever was necessary to give our marriage the best opportunity to flourish.

We began the process of making all the preparations required to make a big move like this. In June 2014 we moved to Springdale and lived in a duplex until buying a home that fit our unique needs. Uncle Keith made the move with us and even lived with us for a couple of years. He was a tremendous help during this time, especially because he worked as my part-time caregiver.

It was during this time that I needed to retire as a Christian counselor because I couldn't work enough to pay for the caregiving, I needed to ensure my wife didn't feel that burden. This was something I said from the start, and I've tried my best to honor that commitment. It took some time to get used to being retired at such a young age, but I decided the caregivers that would come to help take care of me would be my new mission field. Now, I never push my beliefs on anybody but whoever comes here knows I'm a Christian. Hopefully, they can tell by the way I treat them and how I talk to them. I have often become a listening ear and used my counseling knowledge in a friendship kind of way. I also tried to encourage others to follow their dreams even though that sometimes meant losing a great caregiver. I've always enjoyed helping others emotionally so anywhere I find people I try to encourage them.

I have enjoyed our time in NW Arkansas. It has been a respite after 7 years of trials. We have found our rhythm as a family. Thankfully, there have not been the big trials like we experienced early on. We have found a church home that is not afraid to proclaim the inspiration and inerrancy of the Bible. Some Christians believe much of the Bible contains myths and claim we should use human reason and logic when interpreting it. This breaks my heart because once we start picking and choosing what we think makes sense, then truth becomes subjective, and we make our opinions the authority. But God is the only one in authority and His truth is absolute, whether we choose to believe it or not. We are also surrounded by friends who love us and care for us. Our kids are growing and flourishing. I'm sure more big trials will be coming eventually, because that's just life in this fallen world. But I'm going to enjoy the calm as long as it lasts.

As far as my physical health, my body has continued to get weaker, which is the reality of having muscular dystrophy. I pretty much lost the ability to do most things without help over a decade ago. A little over 5 years ago I got a new power wheelchair, and we chose seating that would improve my posture. We didn't realize that it would restrict my ability to drive my chair with my hand. It was starting to get a little difficult anyway, so I chose to look at alternative options. I settled on using a joystick I would control with my chin. It has worked very well, and I have more control with my chin than I had with my hand. The hardest thing to get used to is always having something in front of my chin and constantly in my line of sight. I adapted like so many times before.

About 4 years ago I started having trouble with my voice, because my vocal cords were growing weaker also. This has been a little more frustrating for me. I have always been soft spoken but now it was becoming more difficult to hear me in noisy places. It has now reached the point that I am only able to talk in a whisper. If I am in a group or anywhere noisy, I have to wear a voice amplifier for others to hear me. It's very frustrating at times, especially since I love talking to people. I used to say that if God would give me one thing back, I would ask for the ability to smile. It's true. I am unable to smile due to my FSHD. But now I would ask for the ability to talk louder again. How often we take the little things for granted.

As the years continue to go by, I have no idea what physical loss I will have to deal with next. But one thing is certain, I will continue to lean on the Lord and talk with the people who have been there for me, especially the relationships where I've been able to be Intelligently Vulnerable. I hope you are willing to take the time and make the effort to develop Intelligently Vulnerable relationships yourself.

I have chosen to give you a glimpse into the major events in my life. I wanted you to see how confronting my emotions surrounding my disability changed the course of my life. I have tried to continue to grow and live a lifestyle of Intelligent

Vulnerability. But I also wanted you to see that life is not always easy, even if you courageously venture into Intelligent Vulnerability. Hopefully, you will be better prepared to weather the storm when those trials inevitably come, but unfortunately, there is no way to avoid them.

Intelligent Vulnerability changed my life for the better. Will you have the courage to let it change yours, too?

Acknowledgements

First and foremost, I must give glory to my Lord and Savior, Jesus Christ. My life is under His good providential control. This book would not be possible apart from the story He has given me to share with the world.

I am grateful for the unconditional support of my wonderful wife, Lisa. You have always made me want to be a better man and encouraged me to share my story with others. Your support and commitment to our family has made writing this book possible.

I am also thankful that my kids took the time to read my book and gave me encouragement to keep writing. My daughter, Caitlan, even took the time to email me her favorite quotes and suggestions for improvement in every chapter. Ayden, I know you don't like to read so just taking the time to read it means a lot. You both make my heart burst with joy.

My publishing team helped take my book to the next level. Gene, your advice to shorten the chapters and add a study section helped make my book much more practical. Vera, it was such a pleasure working with you on editing. Your talent is undeniable, and you made my book better and more professional.

I must also recognize Rendi Threadgill for her amazing

design for the front cover and images inside my book.

I lost touch with Jimmie Reed many years ago when he moved to Florida, but I can't thank him enough for the time we spent together working through the early stages of this material and helping me put it in writing over 15 years ago.

Last but not least, I must thank all my family and many friends who have told me how excited they are to read my book. Your support kept me pushing forward.

Made in the USA
Coppell, TX
23 March 2024